Ruinart

the oldest producer
of champagne

from 1729 until today

PATRICK DE GMELINE

Ruinart

the oldest producer of champagne

from 1729 until today

Stock

CHAMPAGNE

SILLERY SUPÉRIEUR

Ruinart Père & Fils

Maison fondée en 1729

RHEIMS.

From Cloth to the Frock

❧ Coronations, wool and sparkling wine.

This trio is indissolubly linked to Reims: the city where the Kings of France were crowned; the city of woollen cloth on which the wealth of various commercial dynasties was based; and the capital of champagne, the wine of kings and the king of wines. And the history of the Ruinart family is linked to all three parts of this trio: to the coronation—it was Irénée Ruinart de Brimont, the most famous member of the dynasty, who in 1825 welcomed Charles X at the gates of the city before his coronation; to cloth, which formed the basis of the family's prosperity; and to champagne, which brought the family a fortune.

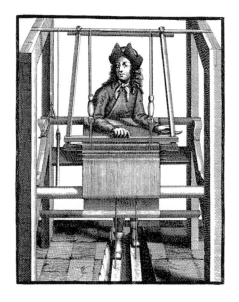

❧ The enduring legend that the Ruinart family

came from Épernay is not in fact true. The first mention of the family is found in Reims in the fifteenth century. The memoir-writer Jean Rogier states that Colesson Ruynart was one of the sixteen citizens of Reims sent to Arras by Louis XI. He was a cloth fuller, and his descendants were to prosper in the cloth trade for three centuries to come.

And they were certainly prosperous: throughout the sixteenth century, numerous legal documents bear witness to the family's prosperity in the form of houses, land and vineyards. The branches of the family involved in farming lived mainly in the town of Beyne, or Beine: Poncelet Ruynart had a house there in 1579, and Jehan Ruynart rented thirteen strips of land there in 1582. Other branches of the family were to be found in Nauroy, Nouchery, Boult-sur-Suippe (where records show that Oudin Ruynart was *lieutenant de justice* in 1663), and in Vaudesincourt; and the commercial branches of the family remained town-dwellers, in Reims, and in the village of Époye.

The merchants Jacques and Jehan Ruynart are also mentioned in Reims

10

in 1604, during the reign of Henri IV. Jean Ruynart, *estaminier*, or muslin producer, rented thirty-seven *septiers* (an old agrarian measure, equivalent to something under 100 square metres) of land at Nauroy. Both lived in the parish of St. Julien and inherited property from their uncle Estienne Ruynart.

So by the middle of the seventeenth century—the century of the Sun King—the family was already well established.

The Ruynarts were cloth merchants, trading in a city whose wealth was based on cloth—a city whose most famous citizen was Colbert, the Sun King's chief minister.

The family line that interests us starts at this period.

Mathieu Ruynart (from this time on, the name was spelt with a "t" at the end, whereas before it had often been spelt with a "d") was born in 1616 or 1617. He was the son of Anthoine Ruynart, who died before 1638, and of Simone Harmonville, who bore her husband two daughters as well as this son. Although contemporary records make no mention of Anthoine's profession, we know that Mathieu was a draper, or, to be precise, a serge merchant. In October 1638 he was apprenticed to Roytelet, a master serge maker, for a period of three years, and a few years later, he became a master himself. He is mentioned in contemporary documents as a merchant, and as a roller and stretcher of serges and muslins. In this century characterised by a love of fine cloths, his business prospered; and in 1656 he bought a house in the Rue Sainte-Marguerite for the sum of 4,000 *livres* from the *sieur* Louis Ballet, a councillor at the Ordinary Court of Appeal in Reims. Ten years later, on 7 September 1666, he made another purchase: this time a fine house in the Rue du Barbâtre in the parish of Saint Martin. Its description still survives: "kitchen, large and small bedrooms, attics, courtyard in front and behind, stables, barns, storeroom, and a garden behind leading onto the the city walls". The façade, on which was hung a sign reading *À la Ville d'Amboise*, was contemporary, but the small gate, with an accolade

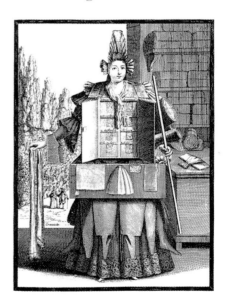

Nicolas de Larmessin: *Linen maid's dress, engraving, end of the seventeenth century. Private collection.*

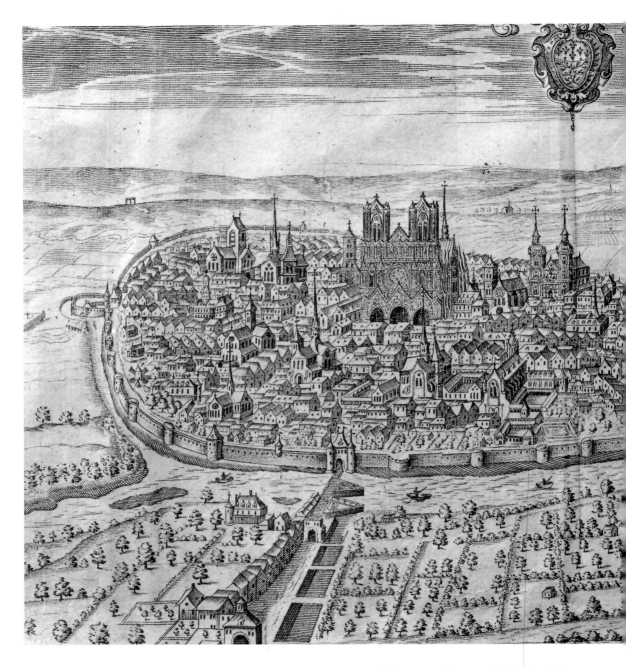

arch on top, was of an earlier period. The part of the building looking onto the courtyard was decorated with a medallion cornice, and inside there was at least one fine chimney-piece, on the ground floor. So this house, bought from the widow Simone Romain for 3,000 *livres*, was imposing enough to be called a *hôtel*. Indeed, Mathieu Ruynart was well-off, even rich, with property to prove it: he owned a house and land at Beyne and at Mouchery, and in 1686 built another house in the Rue

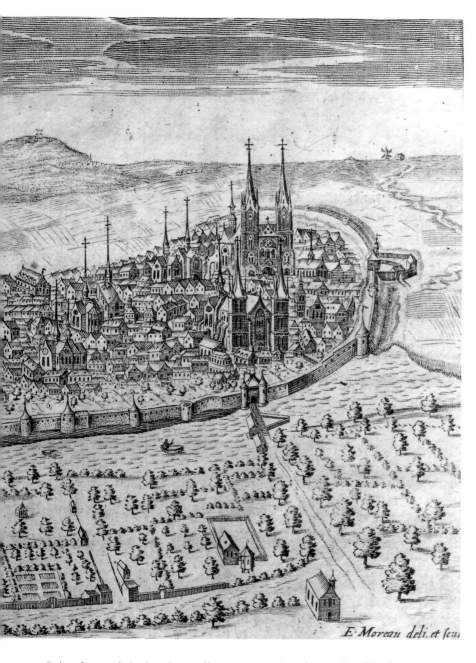

E. Moreau deli. et fcu

Saint-Jean, right by the well-tower, on the city walls. He lived mainly in the house in the Rue Sainte-Marguerite, from where he probably ran his business. He died on 23 March 1702, in the house with the *À la Ville d'Amboise* sign.

There is no mention anywhere of Épernay. The Ruynarts were a respectable Reims family.

And their rise in the world was only just beginning.

13

We do not know more about Mathieu Ruynart, except that at the beginning of 1675, in order to consolidate the dynasty he had founded, he made his son Nicolas a business partner for one year. The contract drawn up on 8 January by the notary Rogier states that father and son "are to become business partners in the trade of serge and muslin, in which they have been involved since October of last year". Mathieu contributed funds of 8,000 *livres* to the partnership, and Nicolas contributed 3,000 *livres*. So Nicolas, aged twenty-three, learnt the trade of wool merchant from his father; and when on 7 August 1676 he got married to Barbe Misson, the partnership was extended for a further nine years.

Did Mathieu Ruynart have an interest in wine? He did possess vineyards, mainly at Berru, but did not exploit them commercially, as his descendants—those of them who remained in trade—were to do. Out of the nine children—seven boys and two girls—from his marriage to Catherine Bernard, two of the boys became priests, and one of the girls, Marie, once she was the widow of Claude Duval, became a nun at Braine.

The second son, Nicolas, carried on his father's activities as *fabricant de rase*, or satin producer.

The last son, Jacques, ten years younger, became Bachelor of Theology at the University of Reims, and in 1686 received from his father the house with the sign reading *À la Ville d'Amboise*, "in exchange for a pension of 500 *livres* during his life, and 50 low masses after his death".

But it was Thierry, the sixth child and fifth son, whose fame was to spread beyond the city and even the province where he was born.

❧ Dom Ruinart (1657-1709), colleague of Mabillon.
The miniature that survives of him shows a thin, almost frail person, drowned in the frock of the Benedictine order, against the book-filled background of his study. He has a pale face whose youthfulness is accentuated by pale eyes and a timid smile under a high forehead topped by a monastic skullcap. He was born in June 1657 and was baptised on the 11 June in the church of Saint-Thimotée. Nine years later he was admitted into the

Anonymous:
portrait of
Dom Thierry Ruinart
(1657-1709).
*Archives Ruinart,
Reims.*
The learned
Benedictine monk is
seated at his desk.
His involvement in
the work of Mabillon,
whose colleague and
biographer he was,
did not prevent him
from appreciating the
value and the future
of the vine.

Bons-Enfants house of the preparatory college for the University of
Reims, and there he began his classical studies. There was nothing
exceptional about this in a family where virtue and religion were part
of daily life. In 1674, when he was seventeen, he became *maître ès arts*,
passing the first university exam.

Even at that period, Thierry Ruinart is recorded as wearing the tonsure,
a visible sign of his religious vocation. But he was not inclined by character to serve in the outside world, as a parish priest. He was, on the
other hand, attracted by the regular life of a monk, and on the 2 August
1674 he entered the Benedictine monastery of Saint-Rémy as a novice.
Less than three months later, on 18 October, he donned the simple
frock, and a year later, on 19 October 1675, he took his vows at the
Abbey of Saint-Faron de Meaux, where he stayed for two years. His
years of study were not over: he pursued his interest in philosophy and
theology at Saint-Pierre de Corbie, in Picardy. And then 1682 was a
major turning-point in his life: his superiors sent him to Paris, to the
Abbey of Saint-Germain-des-Prés, which was one of the main centres of
Christian scholarship. The Abbey was occupied by the Saint-Maur

15

Tombstone of
Dom Ruinart in the
Abbey of Hautvillers:
*"Hic Jacet D. Theode-
rica Rvynart Remensis
Presbiter et Monachvs
s. Germani a Pratis..."*

Benedictines. But most importantly, it was here that the universally famous Mabillon (1632-1707), founder of historical debate, carried out his work. Thierry Ruinart immediately became the colleague of this prominent figure with whom he had so much in common: they both came from Reims; within a few years of eachother, both had studied at the Bons-Enfants and stayed at Corbie. The two men were to develop a deep friendship that was strengthened by intellectual affinities.

For twenty-seven years, Dom Ruinart was to remain the master's disciple, helping with his work, and also accompanying him on his travels, which twice took them abroad: to Germany in 1683, and to Italy in 1685. But most of the two monks' journeys were within France: to Tours, Angers, Clairvaux, and to Alsace and Lorraine. And of course they visited Reims from time to time. In 1696, while returning from Lorraine, Dom Ruinart wrote in his diary: "We travelled down from Sainte-Barbe-de-Versey through a vineyard famous for the quality of its produce." Coming from the Champagne region, Dom Ruinart was far from ignorant about vines.

It was certainly on this occasion that the two monks stopped at the Abbey of Saint-Pierre d'Hautvillers—occupied by the Saint-Vanne Benedictines—not far from Épernay. This brief stay, and another one just before Dom Ruinart's death, gave rise to a tradition for which, it must be said, there is little supporting evidence. We will return to it later. This is not the place to deal with Dom Ruinart's life in detail. But it is worth outlining his achievement. Unlike his master Dom Mabillon, he was far from expansive; he was unadventurous, scrupulous and sincere, with simple tastes, and his studies were his one passionate interest. He had an intimate knowledge of the Classical world, studied the classics in the original, and always had time to stop in front of any tomb or inscription, however unimportant. Based in Paris, he corresponded with the most distinguished scholars of Europe. After Mabillon's death, he started to write his biography, with the support and encouragement of bishops, judges and statesmen—for these people knew Dom Ruinart, the modest monk who was from time to time obliged to tear himself away from the library in Saint-Germain-des-Prés in order to make an appearance at Court. He was even given a small living—the Priory of Saint-Blaise near Noyen. His writings, often in Latin, included several volumes, some of which were published up until the middle of the nineteenth century: *Lives of the First Martyrs*; *Apology for the Mission of Saint Maur*; *The Pallium of Archbishops*—these were the writings of a theologian in the guise of historian, the result of very considerable research. This was all far from the realm of champagne, which cannot in any case have occupied an important place in Dom Ruinart's full intellectual life. He did, however, briefly cross paths with another Benedictine, who played a major role in the history of champagne: this was Dom Pérignon (1638-1715). When Dom Ruinart arrived at Hautvillers during a journey in 1686, Dom Pérignon was acting as steward of the abbey, and so was in charge of the vineyards and storerooms. Although Dom Ruinart doubtless met him, it would be a mistake to think that the two monks

The Benedictine Abbey of Hautvillers. Dom Ruinart stayed there on several occasions, and met Dom Pérignon. He died there one morning in autumn 1709, and was also buried there.

worked together on this subject. For one thing, a brief stay of a few days would not have been long enough; and for another, it is difficult to see Dom Ruinart, the intellectual, being much interested in a discovery that was already twelve years old. In any case, there is a tradition that Dom Ruinart passed on Dom Pérignon's secret to his nephew Nicolas Ruinart, the future head of the family business, who was only twelve when his uncle died, and who cannot have been much concerned with the technical and commercial aspects of wine production.

On the other hand, it is perfectly conceivable that Dom Thierry, being very attached to his family, might have spoken to his brother Nicolas of the enthusiasm shown in Paris and Versailles for the wine of Champagne. And no doubt the family would have listened attentively to the opinion of this monk whom they greatly respected. But it is difficult, against this background, to consider Dom Ruinart to be the father of the future champagne producers.

It seems that he did use his influence to help his family, since in a letter to Dom Ruinart, Daguesseau refers to his brother Nicolas Ruinart as "distinguished warden of the merchants and manufacturers of Reims."

Five months before his death—at the respectable age, for that period, of fifty-two—in 1709, the indefatigable Dom Ruinart had just seen his biography of Mabillon published, and was overseeing the publication of the fifth volume of *The Annals of the Order of Saint Benoît*, as well as wai-

NEXT PAGE

**Jean-François
de Troy:**
Oyster lunch
(detail).
*Musée Condé,
Chantilly.*

From Cloth to the Frock

ting for a new Dutch edition of his *Lives of the First Martyrs*. He decided
to go to Champagne once more in order to consult archives and visit
some old churches. Having spent the month of August at work, he was
preparing to return to Paris, and stopped at the Abbey of Hautvillers.
But there he was attacked by a fever, and took to bed. Seventeen days
later, on 27 September 1709, he died, in spite of the ministrations of the
doctors who rushed from Reims, and the prayers ordered by Gaston de
Noailles, Abbot of Hautvillers and Bishop of Châlons. He was buried in
the choir of the abbey church, under a sturdy tombstone bearing a long
epigraph in his honour.

So died one of the memorable figures of a family that in the next generation were to be the energetic first members of the "champagne aristocracy". No other champagne producer, however many great heads of
family and captains of industry they can count, can boast the presence
of one of the *Grand Siècle*'s most distinguished representatives of historical studies. It is on this count alone that Dom Ruinart must appear in
his family's history, since his influence on the birth of champagne is no
more than anecdote.

At the time of Dom Ruinart's death in 1709, towards the very end of
the reign of Louis XIV, the family business centred above all on cloth.
On a scale that was perhaps less grand, it was comparable to the cloth
dynasties of Lille in Flanders, where considerable fortunes were being
accumulated.

Nicolas Ruinart (1697-1769):
The Birth of Champagne

❦ Two members of the Ruinart
family, father and son, bore the Christian name Nicolas, one after the other. It was the son—Dom Thierry's nephew—who decided to turn the family business away from cloth for good, and towards the wine of Champagne.

Born in 1697, this Nicolas was not the eldest, but rather the youngest of ten children. In the family of Nicolas Ruinart *père* and Barbe Misson, there were five daughters and five sons. One son died when he was one year old, but it seems that the others survived, although almost nothing is known of them. All we know is that Jeanne, ten years older than Nicolas, subsequently married Guillaume Tronson, a merchant of old Reims stock, whose family became famous two generations later when Tronson du Coudray defended Queen Marie-Antoinette when she was tried by the revolutionary tribunal.

❦ "In the name of God
and the Virgin Mary, may this book be begun. 1.7bre 1729." A sentence invoking the help of the Creator and the Virgin, and a date: thus was born the Maison Ruinart, the first producers of champagne. The invocation is at the top of the opening page of a thick volume bound in fawn-coloured leather: an account book from which numerous lessons can be drawn, and belonging to a shrewd and cautious merchant, capable nonetheless of making important decisions affecting not only himself, but also his whole family. He was soon to show these qualities. But that is to look ahead. In 1729, Nicolas Ruinart was still predominantly a cloth merchant. Although this register is the oldest that has survived, it was not perhaps the first one. As M. Decrock so rightly observes in his remarkable economic study of Ruinart based on statistical analysis of accounts, "the fact that there are references to sales made before 1 September 1729 proves that Nicolas Ruinart was not just beginning his career as a merchant."

France was then at the beginning of the reign of Louis XV, although the country was governed by the old Cardinal Fleury, under whose astute financial management commerce prospered. The century of the

Enlightenment had begun and was yet to reach its zenith; and it ushered in an art of living and a refinement which of course affected business.

Nicolas Ruinart started this account book around the time of the birth of his oldest daughter Jeanne, which was followed by the arrival of Barbe Nicole in 1730, Claude in 1731, and Marie Barbe in 1733. These were three years of vital importance, not so much because of the additions to his family, but because they led up to Nicolas' decision, in 1733, to concentrate his resources increasingly on wine—a decision that became definitive two years later.

Until then he had done as his predecessors did, buying and selling cloth, either wholesale or wholesale trade.

The cloth came mainly from Reims and the surrounding region, and Nicolas Ruinart generally sold it on in Paris, Beaune, Reims, or even Lille. Most of his clients were substantial merchants, who in their turn sold the cloth to other clients—retail as likely as not. He travelled frequently on business, and visited his clients at home, or met them at local fairs in Reims—at the "cabbage market" or the "Easter and Madeleine market"—or elsewhere. His merchandise was delivered by his own *roulier* (cart driver), by post coach, or by clients and friends who happened to be going in the right direction.

Nicolas Ruinart traded in cloth; and also in wine—no doubt as his father had done, but in larger quantities. The wine produced in his region was

The first page of the account book of the Maison Ruinart. *"In the name of God and the Virgin Mary, may this book be begun. 1. 7bre 1729."* This is the birth certificate of the oldest producer of champagne.

The Birth of Champagne

well-known: there was *vin de mousse* (sparkling wine) which was not yet an *appellation contrôlée*, and there were also high quality local wines. There were wines from Reims, from the Saint-Thierry *massif*, from la Montagne, and also from la Vallée. Nicolas traded in them regularly. To begin with, he sold both wine and cloth to the same clients. There is however no reason at all to think that the wine was a present, an encouragement to buy cloth, or a sort of thank you: the equivalent of today's free gift or loss leader. Once more, the legend must be seen for what it is: pure legend. Nicolas Ruinart sold his wine—he did not give it away, nor was it part of some special offer. But once in a while he did give some, sparingly, to favoured clients. All the same, the first four years of his account book are almost entirely given over to cloth, with wine as a marginal concern. All this changed in 1733. What happened?

There were two factors.

The first was purely economic. Between 1733 and 1735 prices rose constantly. The rate of increase varied from sector to sector: so that over the following fifty years the price of woollen cloth rose by 22%, whereas the price of wine rose by over 40%. In other words, the eighteenth century was a period of decline for the textile industry, but a period of renewed growth for the wine trade, not only in France, but also throughout the rest of Europe. Although he was no visionary, Nicolas Ruinart was a shrewd businessman with a fair knowledge of economics. He knew that he was making a choice that would be decisive for the future. And as he saw it, he could choose between carrying on in the cloth trade and sharing its declining fortunes, or switching rapidly to wine.

The other (slightly earlier) factor was an administrative decision that gave a decisive stimulus to the trade in wine from Champagne. A ruling of the King's Council of 25 May 1728 allowed the merchants of Reims to transport the wine produced in the region in batches of 50 or

100 bottles; and since they had until then been obliged to transport their wine in casks, this was a small revolution. For the wine of Champagne—for which the production methods had been greatly refined since Dom Pérignon's discovery—had necessarily to go straight into thick bottles plugged with cork. The ruling permitting wine to be transported in bottles allowed the merchants of Reims to deliver their produce anywhere in France, and even abroad. The great adventure of champagne was about to begin in earnest.

Nicolas Ruinart was guided by his instinct; and it was as a businessman that he took his decision. From 1733 on, the buying and selling of wine occupied an increasingly important place in his account book. In 1735 it became the main activity, and the cloth trading activities disappeared bit by bit.

❦ Where did his wine come from?

He did not possess substantial vineyards, although he did own a few small ones, in any case insufficient to meet the demands of his business, or rather, the demands of his clients, which were to increase throughout the remaining forty-odd years of his life. So he bought from local producers—a practice that is still widespread today. About seventy of them appear in his accounts: roughly thirty came from Reims, and the others came from the surrounding area—places like Taissy, Brimont, Chamery, Hautvillers, Écueil, Cormontreuil, Saint-Thierry. There was even an isolated supplier in Burgundy. Nicolas was personally responsible for buying the wine, and visited his suppliers and negotiated prices with them. Sometimes he bought through an intermediary working on commission, like the *sieur* Malatrey who bought for him in Écueil. The standard measure of quantity was the *queue*, a measure specific to Reims, equivalent to about four hundred litres. The size of Nicolas Ruinart's purchases varied considerably, depending on the place of production and the quality.

Of course he had to sell on the wine he bought. But exactly what wine did he sell? At that time there were four distinct varities: *vin ordinaire*, not very highly rated, that sold for about 120 *livres*; *vin nouveau* (one year old), much in demand, that sold for 175 *livres* per *queue*; *vin de la Montagne*, a Reims wine that sold for 190 *livres*; and finally *vin vieux* (two years old) that sold for 195 *livres*. Although the cellarmen of Champagne were skilled, they had not found a means of ageing wine properly beyond four or five years, which explains the varities available on the market. Some of this wine was traded in casks. But only the white wine—sold by the *panier* (basket) of 12, 20, 30 or 60 bottles—was a *vin champagnisé* (in other words, it had undergone the process of *champagnisation*), and its price was much higher.

❦ Who were Nicolas Ruinart's clients?
Most of his Reims clients whose addresses appear in the account books lived in the smart part of the town: evidence of the social cachet already attached to the consumption of champagne. There were similar clients in Lille and Tournai, where Nicolas Ruinart was active and from time to time had storerooms. In Lille, for example, he employed a clerk from 1737 who was responsible not only for sales and deliveries, but also for banking promissory notes. To build up his clientèle, Nicolas made the most of the relationships that he had formed in the cloth trade. Apart from in Reims, most of his wine was sold in the north of France and the south of modern Belgium. Lille was the top of the list, with 67% of sales, and was followed a long way behind by Tournai (12%), and then by a large number of relatively small towns like Cysoing, Cambrai, Charleville, Sedan, Beaupaire and Rethel. Unlike for cloth, there was not much of a market for wine in Paris.

Although some of the abbots and canons to whom Nicolas Ruinart sold wine did nothing to dispel the traditional image of the champagne-loving, *bon vivant* ecclesiastic, his clients also included distinguished laymen, such as a deputy for the Trois États, a surintendant in Mons, a *notaire* (roughly equivalent to an English solicitor) in Cambrai, a professor at the college in Reims, a printer in Paris, the Comte de Sainte-Aldegonde in Tournai, who belonged to one of the most important families in Artois.

Nicolas Ruinart did not deal only with the well-off *bourgeoisie* and a handful of nobles—although these people did form the bulk of his clientèle. He also sold to artisans. For example, his accounts for 1739 record deliveries of wine from Tours-sur-Marne to a tailor, a roofer, a butcher, a carpenter, a baker, a spinner, and a mason. Some of them treated themselves generously, like the carpenter, who bought all of four and a half queues, or 1,800 litres of wine.

The quality of Ruinart's wines was excellent. Proof of this is the fact that most of the wine he sold was delivered to places between fifty and a hundred miles away—sometimes more—and it travelled well. His profits depended on the type of wine: he made 50% on wine from Vernezay; 70% on wine from Taissy; 90% on wine from Brimont; but only 15% on wine from Rilly. M. Decrock's study shows that average net profits were about 39% (between 69,000 and 73,000 livres depending on the year)—figures which alone justify the switch from cloth to wine decided on in 1733.

And by 1736, Nicolas Ruinart had switched entirely to wine, which from now on was his sole business.

Nicolas de Larmessin: *Winegrower's dress,* engraving, end of seventeenth century. *Private collection.*

❦ In the first third of the eighteenth century, the Maison Ruinart was a prosperous business. Nicolas was able to buy a few vineyards, for example at Taissy and Gueux, which he then let out to winegrowers. The accounts show the cost of running these vineyards, especially around the time of the grape harvests, when he bought bottles, corks, candles (Were these part of a parallel business, or were they to finish off the process of sealing the bottles? We do not know.), and even a *cabri* (a kid), in October 1733, doubtless to be roasted as part of the end-of-harvest festivities.

Being a businessman, Nicolas Ruinart of course knew how to manage money. The money which was necessary for the running of his business was entrusted to the care of trusted professional men, bankers who looked after his interests. And although he came from Reims, Nicolas chose to place his affairs mainly in the hands of a Parisian called Jalla-bert, to whom he gave a "crate of very fine wine"; and he also used the services of Raulin Champegnois, a Reims banker who lived in the Rue Porte-Cérès.

It is clear that Nicolas Ruinart was a busy man, personally running his business: we do not know its address, but it was most likely based in his house or not far, in the centre of Reims. Perhaps it was based in the *hôtel* with the sign *À la Ville d'Amboise*, where his grandfather Mathieu had lived and died; or perhaps, again, in the building in the Place de la Ville known as the Hôtel de Joyeuse, which Nicolas doubtless bought, along with other buildings, mainly in the Rue d'Oignon. Nicolas Rui-nart was helped by his wife Barbe, who took control of the day-to-day affairs of the business when her husband was away buying wine or visi-ting his clients. Being a thoughtful husband, Nicolas gave her presents, like the piece of cloth bought in February 1733 from M. Musnier, a dra-per—and also a client of his—in Paris.

But there were breaks from work: the famous account book shows that Nicolas' wine business allowed him to take about two and a half months off work every year, mainly in the summer, when the weather was good, just before the grape harvest. But that habit dates from 1736, for there were years when he did without a break, as in 1731 and 1733.

❦ 1760: thirty years on.
There are almost no records for these thirty years.

But in 1760 Nicolas Ruinart was still in charge of his business, and even more so than before. He was now sixty-three years old—by the stan-dards of the age, an old man. But a fine-looking old man, as the por-trait of him clearly shows: a haughty face under a white wig, full cheeks, a long nose, slightly hooked, pale piercing eyes under dark eyebrows, and a firm mouth. It is the portrait of a man of strong character, quite at ease in his role as founder of a business. He wears a sober black suit against which the white lace jabot only just registers. He is a self-confi-dent *grand bourgeois*.

Over the last thirty years, the Maison Ruinart had expanded and deve-loped. Firstly, Nicolas was no longer alone. In March 1764 he brought in his son Claude as a partner: Claude was then thirty-two, shortly to be married, on 6 May, to Hélène Françoise Tronson, daughter of François Tronson, of an old Reims family. The Tronson du Coudray family will appear later in this story. This marriage brought Claude a dowry of 12,000 francs, which made up three quarters of the total of 16,000 francs that he invested in the family business.

Claude, a wine-trader like his father half a century before, joined a business that had developed considerably. The previous twenty-five years had been mainly spent developing the firm's foreign clientèle.

The times, and also business trends, favoured exporting; although there was no question of the Ruinart business neglecting their traditional clients in the north of France and in Belgium.

Germany was the Maison Ruinart's big new market. There, the wines of Champagne were much appreciated by the numerous greater or lesser princes, and by the nobility in general. And since there were about three hundred and fifty states beyond the Rhine, the market was extensive. To have an idea of the avenues that were open to an enterprising businessman, it should be remembered that a liking for champagne was accompanied, in this century of the Enlightenment, by a generally francophile outlook in the courts of sovereigns and archbishop-princes, and amongst the *haute bourgeoisie*.

Nicolas was certainly enterprising. And he had his son Claude to help him at home in Reims, and also on the long but indispensable voyages abroad to seek out new business. In 1762, for example, he was absent from Reims from mid-April till mid-September, not to mention various journeys in March, at the beginning of April, and in the first half of December. Seven months away from home in one year. The itinerary was admittedly demanding, and is worth looking at stage by stage.

He arrived in Strasburg on 15 May, and the next day he was at Rastadt, on the estates of the Markgraf of Baden-Durlach; and he visited Heidelberg on the 18th, and then went on to Wurtemberg. The 29 May saw him in Stuttgart, the 30th in Ulm, the 31st in Augsburg; and then he returned briefly to Ulm, before going on to Munich, the capital of the Elector of Bavaria. He visited Nuremberg on 21 June, Worms on 8 July, Frankfurt on the 10th, Mannheim on the 17th, Cologne on the 23rd, Liège on the 27th, and, after a journey of over three hundred miles, returned to Guebwiller, not far from where he had started. But it was not yet time to return to Reims. After visiting Germany, he left for the Netherlands. He was back in Amsterdam on 6 August, made rapid visits to Brussels and Gand on the 17th, went to Lille on the 29th, then went to the northern areas, and after passing through Cambrai on 8 September, he finally climbed down from his carriage in Reims.

The next year he set off again, but this time went as far as Berlin, and came back via Würtzburg, Heidelberg, Mannheim, Cologne, Maastricht, Gand, and then, as before, Lille, Cambrai and Reims.

These long business voyages were the last undertaken by members of the Ruinart family until the great journeys to America and Russia in the following century.

From this time on, they sent representatives.

Such effort could not go unrewarded. And indeed the champagne supplied by the Maison Ruinart Père & Fils—the name probably dates from the formation of the partnership in 1764—was drunk by numerous clients, most of whom belonged to distinguished families.

The register of deliveries reads like a list of the noble houses of Europe at the time of the Enlightenment. And it was in 1762—the year of the armistice between Russia and Prussia—that Europe emerged from the Seven Years War, which was to be ended formally the following year by the signing of the Peace of Hubertsburg, and then the Treaty of Paris. Let us begin by looking at Germany, which was to be one of the most important markets—if not the most important—for the Maison Ruinart right up until the First World War. In the last quarter of the eighteenth century, Ruinart sold six times more champagne in the German market than they were to sell there in 1913. Most of the clients there were members of the nobility: in Dresden, Prague, Stuttgart and Mannheim, about 45% of them were noble; and this proportion rose to 76% in Salzburg. Among Ruinart's most distinguished clients were the Markgraf Karl-Friedrich of Baden-Durlach, who reigned at Rastatt and Karlsruhe, and the Markgrafs of Bayreuth, Brandenburg and of Anspach. Bottles of Ruinart champagne were also to be found at the court of Stuttgart, at theWürtzburg residence of the Duke Charles-Eugene of Wurtemberg, at the court of Saxony in Dresden, at the courts of Hesse-Cassel, Brunswick, Lichtenstein and Prague; and at the court in Vienna of Maria-Teresa of Austria, head of the Holy Roman Empire. The dazz-

ling and sumptuous Court in Vienna was of great commercial importance for the Maison Ruinart: numerous German princes—some reigning, others not—were in attendance there. They could enjoy champagne mainly thanks to the hospitality of Prince Charles-Joseph de Ligne (1735-1814), a future Field-Marshal of Austria. Archetypal cosmopolitan *grand seigneur*, spiritual friend of Joseph II, of Catherine the Great, Louis XIV and Marie Antoinette, the Prince de Ligne was one of Ruinart's most distinguished clients: their relationship had started in 1762 in Brussels, the Prince's native town. And it was also doubtless in Vienna, where he was French Ambassador at the beginning of his career, that the Cardinal de Rohan—later sadly notorious as a result of the affair of the Queen's necklace—learnt to appreciate Ruinart's champagne.

Ruinart champagne was also drunk at the Court of the Electors of Bavaria, monarchs of Munich, who were to remain clients the Maison Ruinart until the monarchy fell in 1918.

The most famous client of this period was without doubt Frederick the Great, King of Prussia and friend of philosophers. This enlightened sovereign did not live entirely on a diet of philosophy, military strategy and the works of Voltaire and d'Alembert. He had a liking for the sparkling wine from Champagne—and in Berlin, that meant Ruinart.

Nor were ecclesiastical courts in the Holy Roman Empire entirely abstemious: the Cardinal-Archbishop of Vienna, the Archbishop-Prince of

Anonymous:
Count Colloredo,
Archbishop-Prince
of Salzburg. He is
known to posterity for
his humiliating treat-
ment of Mozart and
for his love of Ruinart
champagne.

Salzburg (Mozart's tyrannical employer), and the Bishops of Trent and Hildesheim all drank Ruinart champagne.

In Hungary, Ruinart supplied champagne to Prince Nicolas Esterhazy, Haydn's patron, to whom the composer dedicated various works.

And in Poland, Ruinart supplied champagne to the Court of Stanislas Poniatowski, who had been elected King by the National Diet under the presidency of Prince Adam Czartorisky.

The Maison Ruinart Père & Fils were also suppliers to William V of Orange, Statthouder of Holland, in The Hague; to Sophie Magdaleine, Queen Mother of Sweden, in Stockholm; and to the King of Denmark, in Copenhagen. Granted their traditional clientèle in the north of France and in Belgium, it was natural that Ruinart should extend activities to these countries. And a client further to the east was the Duc de Courlande, who had pledged allegiance to Russia. But the Russians were not yet clients of the Maison Ruinart, or indeed of any other champagne producer. Champagne was not drunk widely in the Russian Empire until the beginning of the nineteenth century—in the wake of the Napoleonic armies, strangely enough. However, a few great Russian aristocrats did drink Ruinart's champagne. Amongst them was Field-Marshal Prince Nicolas Vassilievitch Repnine (1734-1801), ex-Governor-General of Estonia and Livonia, Ambassador Extraordinary in Poland of the Empress Catherine the Great. An order of his was packed off from Rouen in April 1765, was transported to Danzig, and from then on was supervised by a certain "M. de Rechbunder" (no doubt Rehbinder, heir of an ancient Baltic family), who lived in Russia: his job was to "see to safe delivery".

In Nicolas Ruinart's time, England was only a modest market, with 2% of sales going there in 1762. The relative lack of exports to England was certainly due to the permanent military, diplomatic, colonial and trade struggles in which France and la *perfide Albion* were engaged. But this situation was to change before long.

And how did France fit in? Statistical analysis shows that on average about a quarter of Ruinart's total sales were in France—a proportion that fluctuated according to seasonal variations and economic crises. Unlike their counterparts abroad, distinguished French figures do not feature in the order books for this period.

It would be incorrect to claim that all Nicolas Ruinart's clients were members of the nobility. The statistical analysis carried out by M. Decrock shows that although the nobility formed a considerable part of the clientèle, a wide variety of professions was also represented. In 1762-1763 alone, the Maison Ruinart supplied wine-merchants (mainly in Germany, especially in Breslau, Leipzig, Nuremberg and Dresden— where supplies were also sent to "un café français" (*sic*) in 1764), inn-keepers (in Nuremberg, Bayreuth and Ulm), artisans (many of them in Reims and the surrounding area), financiers (in Würtzburg and Vienna), lawyers, ecclesiastics (mainly in the north of France), and industrialists.

Edmond Leclerq (1817-1853): Charles Joseph, Prince de Ligne (1735-1814). Friend of Catherine the Great, of Frederick the Great, and of Louis XVI, he was one of the most effective "advocates" of Ruinart's champagne in eighteenth-century Europe; he drank it until the end of his life.

🌰 The wines of the Maison Ruinart had changed since the beginning of the century. The old

classifications (*vin vieux*, *vin nouveau*, and *vin ordinaire*) had been replaced by new ones. At the top of the range, there was *vin exceptionnel*, the wine from Sillery, near Reims, a renowned growth: it sold for 750 francs per *queue*. Future generations of the Ruinart family had Nicolas to thank for having bought this famous vineyard a few miles outside Reims. It had previously belonged to the Sillery family, which had a tradition of providing the state with able administrators, and which had provided France with chancellors under Henri IV and Louis XIII. The wife of the Maréchal d'Estrées, *née* Sillery, had been very fond of the wine from this vineyard, which Ruinart sold under the highly-rated *Clos de la Maréchale* label .

Then there were the *vins excellents*, from Beaune and Puisieux. Nicolas made a point of buying Burgundy wines: in 1765 these two sold for 400 and 354 francs respectively per *queue*.

The *très bons vins*, which were next on the scale, came from Épernay, Reims, Châlons-sur-Marne and Aÿ, and sold for between 200 and 230 francs per *queue*. The *bons vins*, which sold for between 140 and 165 francs per *queue*, came from Avize, le Maisnil, Taissy, Plivot, Ambonnay, Oger and Bezannes. The *vins assez bons*, which sold for about

120 francs, came from Villers-Allerand and Chamery. And finally, at the bottom of the range, selling for between 90 and 102 francs—seven times less than the Sillery wine—were the wines from Cramant, Montbré, Rilly, Pierry, Brimont and Cumières.

The Maison Ruinart did not deal only in wines from Champagne and Burgundy: they also sold Tokay—the famous Hungarian growth—as well as Saint-Georges; and in 1768 they even made a delivery of Chambertin to the Prince de Ligne in Mons.

So in the second half of the century, almost all the wine that Nicolas

Ruinart sold was bought from outside suppliers. He bought mainly from the four "key" areas in Champagne. He made almost 40% of his total purchases in the Vallée de la Marne; and a further 40% of his total purchases came from near Reims—20% from the Massif de Saint-Thierry, and 20% again from the Montagne de Reims; and he bought from the Côte des Blancs (10%)—this was a novelty—and from Burgundy. And very occasionally he bought from the Bordeaux region. Nicolas Ruinart did not only buy from Reims and the nearby areas, but he travelled further and further afield in search of ever higher quality.

❧ As a merchant and exporter, Nicolas Ruinart was faced with two problems:

transport and finances. Delivery within France, and especially to far-off destinations abroad, depended on the existence of trouble-free transport routes. Ports and the sea played a vital role, even for deliveries to towns that seemed completely land-locked. Indeed, champagne destined for clients in The Hague, Amsterdam, and even Magdeburg, was sent via Dunkirk; and champagne for delivery in Bremen, Hamburg, and also Frankfurt, left from Rouen. Rivers were a much-used means of transport: the Rhine, the Main and the Danube bore consignments of Ruinart champagne bound for Germany, or for destinations further east; a break in the journey always being essential in Strasburg, which even then played its role as hub of Europe.

Nicolas Ruinart was also a shareholder in the famous French East India Company, that had been founded in 1714. It is possible that he bought his shares acting on advice given by a relation of his wife, the *sieur* Saubinet, who at the time lived in Pondicherry, one of the Company's trading posts, and its main fortified town. Since he did not export to India, Nicolas Ruinart's intentions must have been purely speculative. Had he lived long enough, he would have regretted this investment, but he died a few months before the company went bust in 1770.

The financial side of the business gave rise to correspondence with numerous banks throughout Europe, if only to discount his letters of credit, or to sort out the various problems that typically arose abroad: bad debtors, currency exchange, and even, occasionally, speculation.

Prince Nicolas Esterhazy. He was Haydn's patron, and one of Ruinart's few important clients in Hungary.

Profit margins remained as high in the middle of the eighteenth century as when the business had been founded, 1766 being a particularly
profitable year, with gross margins of almost 45%.

From 1767, Nicolas Ruinart stepped back.

It seems that he looked after the family
vineyards, rather than involving himself directly in the running the
company, which his son Claude increasingly took over. Indeed, in October of that year we see him buying stakes for his vineyards at Taissy;
and on 14 November he bought a house for 12,000 francs.

Five months later, on 10 April 1768, he formally handed over the running of Ruinart Père & Fils to Claude, who undertook to provide his
father with an annual income, from capital, of 55,000 francs: a generous
sum. But he was not to enjoy it for long, for he died in 1769. He had
run his company for thirty-six years: thanks to him, it had expanded
rapidly, a trend that was to continue at an even faster rate under the
management of his son.

Claude Ruinart,
Seigneur of Brimont (1732-1798):
Letters Patent of Nobility

🌣 Full face, high colour,
closely shaved (but clearly with a strong growth), no wig (but
his own hair, powdered), piercing eyes, hint of a smile on thin lips:
Claude Ruinart had the build of a merchant of his times. He lived in
the second half of the eighteenth century, which was to end, in France,
with the Revolution. The portrait belongs to this period. Its subject,
although vigorous, is mature in years. And his clothes are very different from those worn by his father half a century earlier: a difference
that is due not only to changes in fashion, but also to character of the
wearer. Gone are the black coat and white jabot of the *grand bourgeois*
founder of a merchant dynasty, and in their place is a grey frockcoat with
loose collar and large lapel, belonging to a businessman who is used to
travelling, discussing and directing in the style befitting a captain of
industry. The white cravat is subtly offset by a fluted edging, and is
tied with a firm knot, almost *à la diable*. The yellow waistcoat, the
relaxed feel of the portrait, for which the subject has found time to sit,
between one appointment and another: it is a vivid portrayal of Claude
Ruinart, head of his business for twenty-nine years, which were to end
with social upheaval and the collapse of the monarchy.

Yet this forceful merchant was the first *gentilhomme* (in this context, the
term *gentilhomme* refers, quite specifically, to a man of noble rank: the
English term *gentleman* is much looser) in the family. In this respect, he
was a founder; just as his father had been a founder—of his champagne
business.

He had become a partner of Ruinart Père & Fils in 1764, had travelled
on business throughout Europe, contributing to the prosperity of the
business, and had succeeded his father in 1768. Now he was the sole
master on board—although he was subsequently to make partners of
his two sons Irénée and Nicolas. But that is to look ahead.

As a rich merchant, Claude Ruinart naturally had social ambitions. He
had been born a *bourgeois*, even a *grand bourgeois*. Under the *ancien
régime*, in the reign of Louis XV that began in 1770, real respect was
reserved for the nobility; but it was not impossible for families in trade
to acquire the helmet or coronet of nobility. The *noblesse d'épée* was the
preserve of the old nobility dating back to the age of chivalry, and

Crystal flute glass,
eighteenth century.
Normandy.
*Musée des Arts
Décoratifs, Paris.*

admittance to its ranks depended entirely on the King, who could, if he
so wished, ennoble a victorious soldier. But the *noblesse de robe*, on the
other hand, was accessible to families with an adequate fortune; provided, of course, they satisfied various conditions relating to worthiness
and way of life that the King insisted on before he would allow the candidate to purchase an office conferring nobility. So the road was open to
Claude Ruinart, who had the necessary fortune, and a name that had
been known in Reims for two centuries. He himself carried out various
official functions, as *contrôleur des guerres* (inspector for war), and *prévôt
de l'échevinage de Reims*, in other words provost of the merchants—a position that offered proof of the confidence he inspired amongst his peers.
He had taken the first steps; now he needed to see the affair through.
Admittance of the Ruinart family to the *noblesse de la robe* was achieved

Anonymous: Portrait of Hélène Françoise Tronson du Coudray, wife of Claude Ruinart, *seigneur* of Brimont.
Collection of the Comte de Pelet, Château de Courtomer.
This is the portrait of a woman of quality, sister of the man who defended Marie-Antoinette. She furthered her husband's advancement and took part in the affairs of the Maison Ruinart.

in two stages. The first stage was the purchase, on 30 March 1773, of the fief of Brimont and the subsidiary fief of Brimontel. Claude and his wife acquired these fiefs through an exchange of property with the metropolitan chapter of Reims. Negotiations had started three years previously, in 1770. The exchange revolved around two farms on these properties. A feudal condition was attached: the new *seigneur* of the fiefs was to pay homage to the bailiff of the seneschal's court representing the chapter of the Church, which was to retain suzerainty.

The Ruinart family already knew the village of Brimont: in 1735 Nicolas Ruinart had built a house there called *The Hermitage*, which had been destroyed by fire in 1761. The house was now lived in by a master wine-grower who watched over the land that had belonged to the family since the beginning of the century: the property was to consist of over fifty acres in 1789. And not far from the village Nicolas also had a modest country house, which Claude's son Irénée was to replace by a full-sized *château*: but that is to anticipate. For the time being, Claude Ruinart had become owner of the fiefs of Brimont and Brimontel, which both brought with them rent, feudal dues, and the right to exercise three forms of seigneurial justice: *haute, moyenne,* and *basse.* And so he took the title of *seigneur* that accompanied ownership of these fiefs; and in the deeds even added the title of *écuyer* (squire or equerry), which in principle was reserved for noblemen. For the ownership of a fief did not, at that time, necessarily confer the noble status of *gentilhomme.*

It was without doubt for this reason that Claude Ruinart, *seigneur* of Brimont, subsequently decided to purchase an office that conferred nobility: the honorary office of *conseiller secrétaire du roi et couronne de France* (Secretary-Counsellor of the King and Crown of France). It was expensive—several tens of thousands of *livres*—but carried hereditary nobility at the end of twenty years in office, or if the holder of the office died within that period. Having bought his office in 1777, Claude Ruinart de Brimont was therefore due to become a *gentilhomme* (in other words, a nobleman) in 1797—unless, of course, he died before. Unfortunately for him, the Revolution of course made his honorary office obsolete, and if Louis XVIII had not ennobled the Ruinart family under the Restoration, they would have become an example of *noblesse inachevée* (incomplete nobility). But there is no denying that the purchase of the two fiefs and the honorary office of *conseiller du roi* did represent further social advancement for the family. This is reflected in the second portrait of Claude Ruinart, whose title-plaque mentions his status of *conseiller du roi*: the puce-coloured clothes are of high quality, with gold-fringed buttonholes, although the wig does not succeed in disguising the ruddy face of its owner. Claude Ruinart lived and worked in Reims, in the fine Hôtel de Joyeuse that he had inherited from his father. And then in 1782 he bought the large and beautiful Hôtel Metz-Roland in the Rue d'Oignon (which was also called the Rue Monsieur). These two *hôtels*, which in fact formed three houses, were a sizeable ensemble belonging to the same family. But Claude Ruinart must take credit for the extension of the business' commercial premises. It was he who decided to transfer the wine-cellars to above the famous chalk mines of Reims.

Until now, the Ruinart family had found suitable storage space for their wines either in the property they owned—a old document informs us that the cellars of the Hôtel de Joyeuse and the Hôtel de Metz-Montgrand were "vast, and used by the family for their business"—or by renting cellars in the town. Thus, in 1765, Nicolas Ruinart rented a cellar from Canon Ninin, and another one from the carpenter Ganneron. But the expansion of the business created the need for new cellars belonging to the Maison Ruinart outright. Where could these be found?

The Romans had thoroughly worked the underground chalk quarries near the entrance to the town, under the mound of Moulin-de-la-Hausse (also called the mound of Saint-Nicaise). Numerous public and private buildings were and continue to be built with this white stone. The Romans had developed sophisticated extraction techniques, and the shafts went down deep into the ground and formed galleries and connecting chambers—real labyrinths. These chalk quarries had the enormous advantage of being cool and dry, and they stayed at the same temperature and were free from vibrations—in fact they offered ideal conditions for storing champagne. In the eighteenth century they were empty and abandoned, and had not been worked for ages. Claude

Model of chalk quarries, seen in cross-section. The extraction work carried out by the Romans is clearly shown. Model made by M. Guéneau, Châlons-sur-Marne. Archives Ruinart, Reims.

Ruinart therefore decided to buy a part of these quarries and to move his cellars there. He built a series of buildings arranged in a classical formation, and because of their style and layout, they resembled cavalry barracks more than commercial premises. After their destruction in the First World War, they were rebuilt just as before, with their strange appearance intact.

It no doubt seemed difficult to run a business efficiently with the offices and shops at one end of the town, and the cellars containing the stocks at the other end. A capable manager had only to apply simple common sense to the problem—and we have seen that in every generation the Ruinart family had managed to make the right decisions. Nor is it inconceivable that for social reasons Claude Ruinart now wanted to seperate his private residence from his place of business.

So the Maison Ruinart moved to above the chalk quarries at the mound of Saint-Nicaise. They were not to be alone in making this move: they were followed by other champagne producers, some of them bearing distinguished names, like Pommery and Veuve-Cliquot....who are still there.

❦ Then as now,
the way business went depended largely on political
developments. The last decade of the century, marked by the Revolution, was to have considerable repercussions—and less negative than
one might think. Since we possess an almost complete record of orders
and sales for the years 1788-1797, we can accurately assess these repercussions for Ruinart.

It is well known that under the reign of Louis XVI, France enjoyed a
considerable degree of economic prosperity. In spite of several harsh
winters, trade flourished and sales of champagne were buoyant. The
output of the Maison Ruinart rose continually, from 36,000 *cols* in 1762,
to 65,000 in 1789.

Under Claude's management, Ruinart Père & Fils was as export-orien-
tated as before.

The Belgian market, inseperable from the market in northern France,
was already firm, and consolidated in this period.

The nearness of this market meant that Claude was able to see to it personally, without maintaining an expensive network of representatives
and intermediaries. Over the years, this happy situation was to become
less favourable.

The Prince de Ligne was still a faithful client, featuring regularly in the
order book, together with the Duc d'Ursel, to whom deliveries were
made in Brussels from 1776 to 1787, and General de Beaulieu, who also
received a delivery there, in 1791. And still in Belgium, the Duc
d'Aremberg, the Baron de Montmorency, the Marquise de Croy, the
Prince de Graves and the Comtesse de Graves all appear in the order
book for 1792. And in the nearby Netherlands, the Statthouder himself, the Prince of Orange, in The Hague, was a client, as was the Comte
d'Oultremont in Maastricht.

The important development during this pre-revolutionary period was
Ruinart's full-scale entry onto the British market, which really got
underway from 1786. That was the year of the signing of the Eden-
Rayneval Treaty, which lowered the customs duties between the two
countries.

Flute glass in
Viennese crystal,
eighteenth century.
Italy.
*Musée des Arts
décoratifs, Paris.*

Until then, these punitive duties had been set at a minimum of 75% of the value of the goods, and hit wines especially hard, since they were considered a luxury commodity. The resulting prices were prohibitively high. This was a sad loss for a country where wine in general and champagne in particular were much and widely appreciated. But it was the reduction of customs duties that allowed the great majority of British wine-lovers to satisfy their taste not only for Ruinart, but also for French wines in general: in spite of the unfavourable political background, wine exports to England increased ten-fold between 1788 and 1792.

In London, Ruinart delivered to the Duke of York in 1788, the Marquess of Stafford in 1789, the Archbishop of Canterbury, the Duke of Beaufort and the Duke of Cumberland in 1790; as well as to the Polish Ambassador.

It is clear that the initial stages of the Revolution had not yet damaged Ruinart's trade with England; but this was to change before long.

The market in Germany, or rather the Holy Roman Empire, had also changed: it had taken a turn for the worse. To be sure, the most distinguished names were still there in the order books: for 1776 we see the Elector of Mannheim, the Court of Hesse-Cassel, and the Prince Hatzfeld in Breslau; for 1778, Prince Antoine, Duke of Saxony, in Dresden; for 1779, the Count of Schönborn in Vienna; for 1787, the Princess of Lichtenstein and Prince Adam Auersperg in Vienna; for 1789, the Duke Carl of Wurtemberg in Stuttgart and the Count of Metternich-Wuineburg in Coblenz; for 1790, the Count of Holstein in Amberg, Prince Anton Grafsalkowicz in Vienna, and the Prince of Schrautenbach in Salzburg; and for 1791, Princess Cunegonde of Saxony in Coblenz, and the Court of the Elector in Bonn.

But this impressive list of names did not deceive Claude Ruinart: he had only to look through his accounts to see that although demand in Bavaria remained buoyant, the market in the Austrian states, Vienna, Berlin, Dresden and Frankfurt, was declining. Austria was a typical case of the way in which trade depended on politics. The traditional alliance between France and Austria, which had been strengthened by the marriage in 1770 of the Dauphin Louis to the Archduchess Marie-Antoinette, had subsequently weakened. In 1784, Joseph II, in favour of pro-

Collerette, circa 1903. Archives Ruinart, Reims.

tectionism, had imposed high customs duties that had hardly encouraged trade. Nor was this situation confined to Austria: other countries
under her influence, like Belgium, had followed suit. As for Prussia,
which ever since the reign of Frederick the Great had been receptive to
French culture, trade was not exactly on the increase, and diplomatic
relations were strained. Nor was the French Revolution to improve the
situation. On the other hand, the emigration of a considerable number
of French nobles—some wishing only to escape, others to join the
Royalist army—was to result, in 1789 and 1790, in deliveries of Ruinart
champagne to cities such as Coblenz, Bonn, Dusseldorf and Cologne.
The merchants and distributors of the Rhine who now became clients
were to remain so until the First World War.

Four years later, political events once more changed the trade map
of the Maison Ruinart. The newly-born French Republic was now

Antoine Hazart, head cellarman of Ruinart Père & Fils during the second half of the eighteenth century. He worked for Claude Ruinart and his son Irénée. He came from an old family in the Champagne region, and was the first of several generations to be linked to the Maison Ruinart. His descendant Maurice Hazart was the immediate predecessor of Jean-François Barot, the present head cellarman. Contemporary anonymous drawing. *Collection of the Comte de Moulliac.*

isolated by a coalition that had brought together Prussia, Austria, England, Russia, Holland, Spain, Sardinia, and numerous German principalities. Foreign armies were at the frontiers, and the English navy was imposing a blockade on the ports—all of which had the immediate and concrete consequence of putting a stop to the flow of exports towards Germany, England, Holland and the north of Belgium. It was a hard blow for a business whose success had been based for the last three centuries on exports.

Nor were the obstacles to trade entirely the result of hostile foreign action the international political situation—new French laws also played their part. The liberalism of 1789 was followed by a policy of protectionism that resulted in a serious economic crisis in 1792-1793. The wine trade was also affected. And on top of this was the famous phenomenon of the *grande peur* (great fear) that resulted from the danger of travelling on the roads within France, the English naval blockade, and the war on the frontiers in the north. It is no surprise that the Maison Ruinart's account books for this period do not show any exports to England or the Holy Roman Empire.

The only region where champagne sales were not affected, indeed where they even increased, was eastern Europe. Poland features in the order books for this period, with clients mainly in Warsaw, Cracow, Grodno, Stettin and Gdansk. Russia had not yet become an important market, in spite of the expeditions to Riga, an important port on the Baltic, and capital of Livonia, one of the Baltic states that was an integral part of the Russian Empire. But the two clients recorded for St. Petersburg in 1775 were prestigious, and were to be instrumental in the choice of Ruinart as suppliers to the Court. They were Count Roman Vorontzov (1707-1783), General-in-Chief, *aide-de-camp-général* to Catherine the Great, and Senator; and his son Count Alexander (1741-1825), ex-Minister Plenipotentiary in London, current Privy Counsellor, and also President of the College of Commerce. He was to become Chancellor of the Empire and Foreign Minister in 1802, and was to win fame as a scholar and translator of the works of Voltaire. His sister was the famous Princess Dachkov, President of the Academy of Sciences, and the main instigator of the arrival on the throne of Catherine the Great. It is nice to think that she must have drunk Ruinart champagne in her brother's palace in St. Petersburg. Another client of the Maison

Ruinart in the Russian capital was Count Johann-Eustache von Goertz (1737-1821), a distinguished Prussian diplomat, then ambassador of Frederick the Great to the Court of Catherine the Great.

Flute glass with stem decorated with sea horses. Sixteenth century. *Musée des Arts Décoratifs, Paris.*

❧ Let us pause for a moment. In 1794, France was in the midst of revolutionary turmoil.

This was the period of the Reign of Terror, coming after the executions of Louis XVI and Marie-Antoinette—and also of Danton. The fall of Robespierre, on 9 Thermidor, marked the end of a bloody chapter.

The Ruinart family kept out of the political upheavals, but the position of Claude Ruinart de Brimont, former *conseiller secrétaire du roi* and *écuyer*, known to be both Catholic and monarchist, clearly marked him out for condemnation before long by the *sans-culottes* of Reims.

Claude Ruinart kept a low profile. But he was a prominent figure, and his monarchist sympathies were no secret in Reims. And was his wife not the brother of Philippe Tronson du Coudray, a lawyer in one of the pre-revolutionary *parlements*? Indeed, his brother-in-law was to win his place in history by defending the unfortunate Queen Marie-Antoinette from her accusers in the *Convention*—for which he was arrested as he left the courtroom.

Claude Ruinart refused to emigrate, as he was apparently urged to do by several of his friends. In spite of his family's concern, he was induced to stay where he was by his age, his health, which was no longer so good, and the popularity that he had earned in the course of the years—apart from anything else, he was chairman of the governing body of the *hôtel-Dieu*. His family consisted of his four children and, of course, his wife Hélène Tronson—the "du Coudray" was to be added by her brothers, Guillaume, the lawyer, and Philippe, a general in the artillery, and fellow-soldier of La Fayette during the American War of Independence, and by the *abbé* Tronson, Father Superior at Saint-Sulpice. Of the children, Charlotte, the oldest, died at a young age in 1779. The next child was Nicolas, born in 1765, who was later to take the title of *seigneur* of Les Fontaines and marry Françoise van der Veken; he was a partner of the family business from 1794, but does not seem to have been much

Germain: portrait
of François Irénée
Ruinart, Vicomte de
Brimont (1770-1850),
Mayor of Reims,
Deputy for the Marne,
Gentleman of the
King's Bedchamber.
*Collection of the Comte
de Pelet, Château
de Courtomer.*
His achievement was
second only to that of
his grandfather
Nicolas, the founder
of the family business.

Flute glass in Venice
crystal. Eighteenth
century.
*Musée des Arts
Décoratifs, Paris.*

Letters Patent of Nobility

involved in its expansion. Marie-Hélène, born in 1767, had been married to Antoine de Maillefer since 1788. And finally, François Jean Irénée, the youngest, born in 1770, was to carry on the tradition of the house, in whose business he had been active since about the age of twenty. He had become a partner on his marriage in 1790.

So Claude Ruinart carried on running his business, concerned mainly to avoid the dangers of the time. One of these was counterfeit currency. In December 1792 he handed in to the town council a forged *assignat* for 300 francs, which he had no doubt received from a thoughtless client. It was the second incident of the kind that year: in June, Claude Ruinart had been given a counterfeit note, this time for the sum of 1,500 francs. Problems of this sort did not arise for sales made abroad, which were paid for in the currency of the relevant country: the florin in Germany, the pound in England, the crown in Austria. But exports picked up —slowly—only in the spring of 1795, and in 1797 in the case of England: one of the economic results of the new Constitution of Year III, enacted in 1795, which marked a return to liberalism.

Claude Ruinart was now no longer involved in the day-to-day running of the Maison Ruinart Père & Fils: his sons François Irénée and Nicolas —but mainly the former—had been in charge since the partnership agreement of 16th June 1794.

He retired from business life, but no doubt kept an eye on the progress of the business that he had helped to build up—and whose activity started to pick up again in 1795. But he was no longer the main decision-maker.

On 2 May 1798—or, to use the calender of the French Revolution, 13 Floréal of the Year VI—he died in his house in the Rue d'Oignon. His widow was to survive him for more than a quarter of a century. He had reigned over the Maison Ruinart for twenty-nine years, and left it in good hands.

❧ Mayor, Deputy and Viscount... three titles for one man.

François Jean Irénée de Ruinart succeeded his father Claude in 1794, and was to rule over the Maison Ruinart Père & Fils for thirty years.

He was born on 30 November 1770 and was baptised the next day in the church of Saint-Michel. His godfather was Jean Quérangal de Guéroisies, the King's revenue collector for Reims, and his godmother was Barbe Nicole du Terre, *née* Ruinart, who was also his aunt. When he was still very young, his father sent him to attend the Benedictine college at Douai, where he studied the humanities. But these did not consist only of Latin, Greek, French and maths. Claude Ruinart intended that his son should be a competent businessman, capable also of conducting business abroad. Irénée—of his three Christian names, this was the one that he was called by—therefore studied English and German: so we are informed by his grandson and biographer Thierry-Amédée, Sub-Prefect of Cosne-sur-Loire.

Germain: Portrait of Brigitte O'Garvey, Vicomtesse Ruinart de Brimont, and wife of François Irénée. *Collection of the Comte de Pelet, Château de Courtomer.*

These wide-ranging studies were soon over: to quote his own words, "I started to help my father at the age of sixteen [in 1786]. I travelled on business." As well as travelling, he supervised the running of the family's properties. Claude Ruinart de Brimont was kept busy by his many duties, and was glad of the help of his sons Nicolas and Irénée.

It was natural that his travels should lead to new acquaintances. And in Rouen, in 1789, he met Robert O'Garvey, *écuyer* and judge in the town's commercial court, as well as his wife, and, more importantly, their daughter Marie Elisabeth Brigitte. He married her the next year: he was not yet twenty. As their name suggests, the O'Garveys did not come from Normandy, but were of Irish extraction. They were one of the noble families that had come to France in 1688 with the exiled James II, King of England and Scotland, and a convert to Catholicism. Irénée was now allied to an old family, prominent in Rouen, and closely related to the English aristocracy. This was therefore an excellent marriage that could do no harm to the future development of Ruinart's affairs in England. But for the time being, Irénée had to face the realities of the French Revolution, a turbulent period socially, politically and commercially. He lived through it beside his father and brother; and showed such outstanding business acumen that his father allowed him ever greater autonomy. His influence began to increase in the business in which, following a by now firmly established tradition, he had taken a 25% stake at the time of his marriage.

Like the rest of his family, but more so that his father, who in some matters sympathised with Voltaire, Irénée was a Catholic and a Royalist. In Reims, he often did what he could to prevent acts of revolutionary excess against people and property, and he travelled to Paris several times to meet and confront members of the Convention. The customs of the times were not respected in the Maison Ruinart: the term *citoyen* (during the Revolution, *citoyen*, or citizen, replaced the more formal and hierarchy-conscious *monsieur*) appears in the account books only seventeen times between July 1794 and Jaunary 1796.

In 1794 Irénée became controlling partner in the family business, with five eighths of the capital (his father kept a quarter of the partnership, and his brother Nicolas had only one eighth), and from then on he ran the Maison Ruinart Père & Fils.

❦1796: for one year the Directory had been ruling France in the place of the Jacobins.

The armies of the Republic under Moreau and Jourdan were occupying Munich and Frankfurt. Austria had become the main enemy, that the Directory was attempting to defeat by signing alliances or treaties of neutrality with Spain, Sardinia, Bavaria, and Wurtemberg. Bonaparte, the Corsican general who since May had been at the head of the French army in Italy, was achieving a series of successes. In 1797 French forces in Germany were once more on the advance, and in October of that year Bonaparte signed the Treaty of Campoformio. The French were now in control of the Austrian Netherlands and almost the whole of Italy.

All this military activity had consequences for trade. Ruinart's champagne could once more be exported to Germany and Vienna. The flow

**Bottle-label from
the Maison Ruinart.
Archives Ruinart,
Reims.**

of orders started again. In Berlin, the Prince Royal of Prussia, the Princes Ferdinand and Louis, the famous Princess Louise who lived in the Radziwill Palace, and the Prussian Court; the Elector of Bavaria in Munich, the reigning Prince of Meiningen, the Elector of Hanover in Passau, the Count Fersen in Carlsruhe, the Prinz von Thurn und Taxis, the Prince of Hohenlohe in Breslau, the Elector of Trier in Augsburg, and the Prince Birkenfeld in Munich. In Vienna, the Princess of Lichtenstein-Oettingen, the Duke Ferdinand of Wurtemberg, the Prince de Ligne, the Prince Lichnovski and the Princess Lubomirska; and in Salzburg, the Archbishop-Prince and the Governor, the Prince of Chiemsee. Irénée Ruinart—and could his Irish marriage have influenced him?—re-established commercial relations with England, which had been at war with France since the beginning of the Revolution, and was imposing a sea blockade. This blockade was not completely impermeable, but all the same despatches to England were rare. Commercial relations had been restored with Belgium, somewhat tentatively, and also with the Netherlands, which had recently been annexed.

❦ Five years later, the situation had changed considerably. 1801 was the second year of the Consulate, headed by Bonaparte. The Treaty of Lunéville was signed, bringing peace with Austria, and, soon after, with Russia. And in 1802 the Treaty of Amiens secured peace with England. The Bank of France had been founded in 1800 (the Maison Ruinart immediately made use of the various financial advantages that it offered), and the *Code civil* had been completed.

General peace brought general prosperity. Trade started up again, exports were encouraged, imports were subject to restrictions, and inflation was now under control. The city of Reims obtained permission to set up a chamber of commerce. It consisted of eight local manufacturers and a wine merchant: Irénée Ruinart, who saw no reason not to make the most of the opportunities offered by peace.

And Irénée did not fail to exploit these opportunities. For the Maison Ruinart, the Consulate was, by a considerable margin, a time of unprecedented prosperity.

Let us take a look, first of all, at the French market, which expanded as never before. Sales, which had previously been confined to the north, near Belgium, now began to advance towards the south, where Marseille, Montpellier, Aix-en-Provence and Nîmes paved the way to Italy —where new markets were now established in Milan, Venice and Palermo. In all this there was nothing surprising, since the victories of France's armies opened new avenues for *voyageurs*—the commercial travellers who traditionally arrived in the wake of soldiers.

The almost total disappearance of customs duties for exports to Belgium allowed the Maison Ruinart to expand its presence there. There were now clients, in Liège, Verviers, Luxemburg, Neuf-Château, Bouillon, and Marche-en-Flamenne. And Ruinart's *voyageurs* also found new clients in Alsace, Lorraine, Franche-Comté, and in the Vosges, as well as in Strasburg, Metz, Nancy, Toul, Épinal, Rambervillers, Saint-Dié, Besançon, Dole, and Dampierre. Nor were these Ruinart's only new markets: the list included Picardy, Burgundy and the Lyonss area. At a time when sales in France were buoyant as never before, the foreign market was also coming along very well.

Germany, Austria, Belgium, Italy and the Netherlands have already been mentioned. And although the naval blockade prevented the Maison Ruinart from asserting its presence in the English market, it did not prevent the Prince of Wales himself, the Duke of Bedford, the Duke of Somerset, the Marquess of Salisbury, Lord Chesterfield, the Earl of Essex, the Marquess of Hartsford and Lord Mansfield from obtaining supplies of Ruinart champagne between 1801 and 1803. The Eastern European market was expanding, too. In Warsaw, there were several clients among the Polish aristocracy; and the furthest market to the east was St. Petersburg, hesitant for the time being, but offering hopes of future expansion.

Bottle-label from the Maison Ruinart. *Archives Ruinart, Reims.*

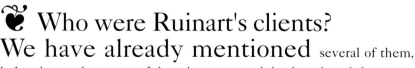 Who were Ruinart's clients?
We have already mentioned several of them, belonging to the cream of the aristocracy, mainly abroad: and they were decisive in creating Ruinart's image. But under the Consulate and the Empire, the social and professional mix of the clients changed considerably.

Mayor, Deputy and Viscount

There exists a detailed study for the year 1802. Out of a total of 739 sales, we can identify 422 clients by category. At the top of the list are wine merchants (26.5%), followed by restaurant-owners, caterers, inn-keepers and hoteliers (24.2%), members of the nobility (12%), lawyers and financiers (11%), doctors and pharmacists (8.4%), civil servants (8%), and army officers (6.4%). And then there are ecclesiastics, industrialists, farmers and artisans. In short, compared to the previous survey for 1762, forty years before, the proportion of total sales going to certain categories of client had fallen—nobility down 16%, ecclesiastics down 9.6%, artisans down 6%—whilst other categories were now buying a greater proportion of total sales than before—notably the food and hotel industry, with a 14% increase. And for the first time clients included army officers, managers of drinking establishments, doctors, surgeons, pharmacists and farmers.

Ruinart champagne was selling more amongst the professional classes, including amongst clients who acted as intermediaries between Ruinart and a less aristocratic, more *bourgeois* clientèle than under the *ancien régime*. But it would be a mistake to generalise, since the different categories were represented more in some towns than in others. For example, civil servants made up 100% of the clientèle in Vesoul and Colmar, and 50% in Épinal; army officers formed the greater part of the clientèle in the east of France, where there were garrison towns like Strasburg, Besançon, and Metz; financiers were an important group of clients in Lyonss and Paris—the two main economic centres of France— as were wine merchants in Marseille, Courtrai and Liège (or the north in general), and in Belgium.

The clients in Paris lived mainly in the smart neighbourhoods in the centre. And in London the deliveries were mainly made to addresses in the aristocratic residential areas of Mayfair, Piccadilly and Oxford Street, all in the West of the city; although some deliveries were made further east, to the offices of trading houses in the City, which had been London's business and finance centre since the beginning of the eighteenth century.

So the clientèle abroad remained mostly aristocratic, and in France was increasingly made up of members of the upper and middle *bourgeoisie*. But in spite of his Royalist views, Irénée was happy to sell to those who

Doit — **Bonaparte** 1er Consul de la — Republique française à **Paris** — **Avoir**

16	22	à Compte de Vin	£	5280		30	8	par Vernier & Cie	£	5280		
28	133	à Compte de Vin		1.104		11	147	par Vernier & Cie		1.104		

Merlin Place Vendôme — à **Paris**

7	42	à Compte de Vin	£	480		30	100	par Vernier Cte Courant	£	480	
16	224	à Compte de Vin		300		30	281	par Vernier Cte Cie		300	

S.E. Mgr De Talleyrand Ministre — Relations Extérieures Rue du Bac Hôtel Gallifet à **Paris**

7	43	à Compte de Vin	£	300		23	C476	par Vernier & Cie	£	900	
24	36	à Compte de Vin		8550		14	147	par Vernier & Cie		1.012	10
27	57	à Compte de Vin		960		1	C509	par Banque de France		2.797	10
3	207	à Compte de Vin		975		14	C518	par Doret		1.012	10
						21	C536	par Banque de France		2.025	10
						4	C559	par Banque de France		1.012	10
						12	C557	par D.		1.012	10
						11		Balance à l'Extrait G 8 143		1.150	
			£	11935					£	11935	

Doit L'Archevêque D'York — à **Londres** — **Avoir**

1797 Avril 15 16 Aria à jour doze Bouteilles — Sept 14 14 £ 355 15 — 1797 Juillet 1er pour Balance à l'Extrait de Nouvelle Société — Sept 14 14 £ 312 16

Le Clerq Menuisier et Md de Vin à la Manufacture à **Guise**

1811						1812					
Novembre 23	à Compte de Vin	f 345 f	80			Juillet 1er	Balance à l'Extrait J	f 220 f	80		

Kockaert Ancien Conseiller près Ste Gudule à **Bruxelles**

1806						1807					
23	à Compte de Vin	f 153 f	242	10		Janvier 31	par Bernard	f 196 f	242	10	
14	au dit	180	600			Mars 31	par ant Van Cuik nije	206	600		
17	au dit	167	330			Avril 30	par le dit	183	330		

S. M. L'Impératrice Reine

1806						1807					
23	à Compte de Vin	f 414 f	225			Février 28	par Cuik heim	f 192 f	466		
5	au dit	168	241			Novembre 30	par le dit	139	210		
16	au dit	95	542 8			Juin 30	par Profit et perte	203	524 5 3		
31	à Vernier	105	191 17 3								
		£ 1200 5 5?						£ 1200 5 3			

were in power, whether they belonged to the new order or the old. His most illustrious client was also the head of state: Bonaparte, the First Consul. And Bonaparte's brothers followed suit: Louis, future King of Holland, but for the time being Brigade General in Compiègne, and also Joseph—both were clients.

And then there was the Minister of Foreign Affairs, the famous Charles-Maurice de Talleyrand-Périgord, who was to remain a faithful client. On 7 Brumaire of the Year XII (30 October 1803), he received the following letter in his residence, the Hôtel de Gallifret:

"We have the honour of providing you with information about this year's vintages. We are most happy to be able to state that this year our wines are of the very best quality. They are strong, with a good nose, will keep well, and will certainly mature excellently. M. Ruinart de Brimont will have the honour of seeing you this winter and of putting ourselves at your disposal. We beg you to continue to put your trust in us, and to believe that we will do everything in our power to deserve it. We have the honour to be Your very humble and obedient servants Ruinart Père & Fils"

Commercial letter sent to the Prince de Talleyrand by Ruinart Père & Fils.
Archives Ruinart, Reims.

❦ On 18 May 1804 the Empire replaced the Consulate. Would France's new régime bring the same remarkable level of prosperity to the Maison Ruinart as they had recently enjoyed?

In any case, Irénée Ruinart did not hide his hostility towards the Empire. Out of all the positions of responsibility in Reims that were his for the taking, he accepted only one, as elected member of the newly-formed *conseil général* of the Marne region. In this post, his experience and knowledge of commerce and industry were invaluable. Otherwise, he devoted his time to his own affairs, which were complicated by France's relationship with the rest of Europe.

The years 1805 and 1806 saw the formation of new coalitions that united England, Russia, Austria, Sweden and Prussia against Napoleon. England once more imposed a naval blockade on French ports, and Napoleon reacted by imposing the Conintental Blockade banning all commerce with England and her representatives. All English ships

were searched by the French navy, and the same applied the other way round, so that there was a complete freeze on sea traffic.

Like other champagne producers, Ruinart was directly affected by this state of affairs. That was the end of exports to England—in spite of Irénée's family links, which all the same must have made it easier for him to put his sons down for English boarding schools—and also of sales in the German market. There was no question of sending goods via the Baltic Sea and the North Sea to countries with which France was in any case almost permanently at war.

So for the time being Irénée Ruinart fell back on the French and Belgian markets, where he initiated a determined sales drive.

His salesmen—there were about ten of them—went from Bayeux to Strasburg, from Normandy to the Pays-de-Loire, and travelled around Picardy, Thiérache, Lorraine and the Vosges. They visited medium-sized towns, small ones, and even villages: Ruinart champagne was brought to the attention of every potential client in France, and was sold throughout the country. It was a new way of doing business: the salesmen searched out orders in almost every region, with the possible exception of Bretagne.

During these years of France's isolation, Irénée Ruinart also directed his attention towards Luxembourg and the surrounding area, which lay on the route to Belgium, an old client. The commercial staging points of this "Ruinart route" were Vouziers, Montmédy, Victor, Marche-en-Famenne, Bastogne, Arlon and Luxemburg, before branching off towards Namur, Liège, and the canton of d'Aubel.

Various distinguished names added lustre—if that is what one can call it —to the list of clients: Murat, then Governor of Paris (who as Grand Duc de Clèves was to remain faithful to Ruinart, if not to Napoleon), and also General Junot and Marshal Lefebvre. As for members of the *ancien régime* who were now serving the new order, the list, as we have already seen, was headed—perhaps not surprisingly—by the Prince de Talleyrand-Périgord, Minister of Foreign Affairs. Then—to quote a few of the better-known names—there were the Bishop of Arras, Monseigneur de la Tour d'Auvergne, the Duchesse de Choiseul and the Comtesse d'Oultremont, who was in any case more Belgian than French. The world of diplomacy was represented by the Marchese Lucchesini, who, in spite of his Italian name, was in Paris as Prussian Ambassador, and by the Prince of Nassau-Siegen. In 1806, the name of the Empress-Queen herself was added to this list.

But Irénée Ruinart definitely belonged to the political and religious opposition: he entertained Cardinal Consalvi and Cardinal Brancardo, who opposed the policies of Napoleon's Concordat. He even paid them allowances, which in their eyes replaced the allowances offered to them by the Imperial government.

1809: the Continental Blockade was now less strictly imposed, for both political and economic reasons. The political reason was that Louis Bonaparte, now King of Holland, had opened his frontiers to trade with England. And the economic reason was that France's agricultural prosperity, largely due to a series of good harvests, forced the government to make various exceptions to the ban on trade with England. And so in 1810 a system of trading permits was introduced, and some of these were granted to wine-merchants. But it was only in February 1812 that the Maison Ruinart resumed deliveries to London and Dublin. Deliveries to Rotterdam increased rapidly; but the German market was very slow to open up again, largely because of the military operations which turned the country into a battlefield and of course tarnished the image of France and her goods. Mainly with the help of his numerous banking contacts beyond the Rhine, Irénée Ruinart settled accounts by arranging for previous deliveries to be paid for in Vienna, Regensburg, Munich, Prague, Frankfurt, Breslau, Karlsruhe, and Dantzig. Clients often asked for extension of credit, and some debts were not paid off until 1821, or even 1836: so after the years of the Empire, the German market recovered only very slowly.

❦ It was the year 1814, and the Cossacks were in Reims. The fierce horsemen of the Imperial Russian army arrived with the Allies, who faced Napoleon in the short but—for France—glorious campaign that was fought mainly in Champagne. The Emperor was fighting for his survival, but his victories at Champaubert, Montmirail, Vauchamps, Montereau, and Berry-au-Bac kept his enemies at a respectful distance.

On 13 March, having defeated the Russians at Champigny and ousted the Prussians from Cormontreuil, near Sillery, he entered Reims, which was lit up for the occasion. Accompanied by Marshal Ney, Prince de la Moskowa, Napoleon went that very evening to the Château du Grand Sillery, owned by Irénée Ruinart de Brimont. He dined on "cold fowl" (so we are informed by Amédée de Brimont), spent the night there, and doubtless drank some of the champagne produced by his host, perhaps one of the famous *Clos de la Maréchale* vintages. The Emperor knew and liked Ruinart champagne: he features in the order books for the period when he was an ordinary general under the Directory. We do not know whether Irénée was present that evening, but it is most probable that he was eager to welcome the Emperor personally, in spite of his lack of sympathy for the Empire. A few weeks later, Reims was occupied. Strangely, this occupation by foreigners brought new clients for Ruinart and the other champagne producers: they were the Russian and Prussian officers, whose tastes were refined, and who were lovers of good food and fine wine. The champagne flowed. French Society saw their presence as a sign of the imminent arrival of Louis XVIII and the Bourbons.

Irénée Ruinart went up to Paris, where events were being decided. The Maison Ruinart delivered supplies of champagne to the Royalists, like the famous Duchesse de Duras, wife of the principal Gentleman of the King's Bedchamber, hostess of one of the most brilliant literary salons of the Restoration, and known to posterity as the chaste and fervent admirer of Chateaubriand. Another client was the Count of Casabianca, previously a general, Governor of Genova, and Senator of the Empire, and subsequently, having rallied to the Bourbons, *pair de France* (in the Constitutions of 1814 and 1830, a member of the upper house, or *Chambre des pairs*.) Ruinart champagne was also supplied to some of the famous foreigners who for a while lived in Paris, which had become the capital of Europe, due to the presence there of the Tsar Alexander, King Frederick-Wilhelm of Prussia, and the Emperor Francis of Austria: clients included Prince Wilhelm, heir to the throne of Prussia and future Emperor of Germany (in 1870) under the name of Wilhelm I; and, more famous still, the great Duke of Wellington, commander of the Allied forces, who was to defeat Napoleon at Waterloo in the following year.

Belloni: picture of the Maréchale d'Estrées, commissioned by Ruinart Père & Fils and reproduced on the labels of the *cuvée* that was named after her, the Clos de la Maréchale.
Archives Ruinart, Reims.

🍇 1815: the Restoration. For Irénée Ruinart, the return of the Bourbons was an undiluted blessing: politically,

because he could now openly express his Catholic and Royalist views; and commercially, because he was able to expand his business, which, in truth, had not suffered a great deal under the Empire. In June of that year, all the important crowned heads of Europe assembled for the Congress of Vienna. And there, in the capital of Austria, Ruinart champagne was served at the table of Lord Stewart, the English Ambassador to the Austrian Emperor. In Paris, a distinguished client was François-René, Vicomte de Chateaubriand, a Royalist if ever there was one, diplomat, minister, but most of all a writer—although in his *Mémoires d'outre-tombe* he hardly mentions Ruinart champagne. And in London, the Duke of York and the Duke of Cambridge also drank Ruinart champagne.

Irénée Ruinart spent as much time in Paris as in Reims, organising his sales, supplying champagne to the Court and the town, and also to the *faubourgs*, via the restaurant-owners and wine-merchants whose clients there were celebrating the return of the Bourbons—or drinking nostalgically to the Empire, or even to the Republic. And the new Bourbon King, the gout-ridden but well-read Louis XVIII, intended to acquire the support of everyone who counted in France. No doubt this explains the order dated 24 July 1815 naming Irénée Ruinart de Brimont as president of the electoral college of the Reims *arrondissement*. And that same year he was made a Chevalier de la Légion d'Honneur. These were the first steps towards his election as Deputy—and indeed he was confirmed as official candidate on 14 August. The voters of Reims approved his candidature and in 1816 sent him to represent the town in the Chamber of Deputies, which was nicknamed the Chambre Introuvable because of its overwhelming Royalist majority. And now, with his entry into parliament, a new chapter in his life began— although it must be admitted that his distinguished performance in office did prevent him from concentrating on his business as before. The King's government showered him with honours; and on 12 April 1817, Louis XVIII signed his letters patent of nobility, thus putting an end to the strange situation of *noblesse inachevée* which had arisen because the Revolution had, as we have seen, prevented his father

Claude from occupying the office of *conseiller secrétaire du roi* for the necessary period of twenty years. At the same time, Irénée Ruinart received a coat of arms, which are illustrated on the document now in the Maison Ruinart's archives: "Azure background with gold chevron pointing upwards, with a silver star on either side and a silver heart underneath; and above, a rose on a gold background. Two lions bearing the shield."

Views of M. Ruinart de Brimont, Deputy for the Marne, on the "Voies et Moyens" bill. He delivered his speech in the Chamber of Deputies on 30 June 1819.
Archives de la Marne.

🥂 Sitting on the centre-right, Irénée Ruinart de Brimont was not an *ultra*, but he

made no effort to conceal his pure Legitimist beliefs. He had no intention of being a passive participant in the process of government, and he was appointed a member of the accounts committee in the new parliament. This is not the place to describe his duties in detail: let us just say that until 1821 he played an active role in parliamentary life. As member of several committees, he took part in numerous debates on bills concerning army recrutement, finances, trade, tax, and generally anything to do with the economy. In 1818 he took up the cause of the friars working in Christian schools, and managed to get them exempted from military service, like the pupils of the École Normale, who were training to become teachers. But this intense activity did not prevent him from being beaten in the elections of October 1821.

He returned to Reims. He was no doubt disappointed, but received the consolation of a job that was much more important for his career and the standing of the Ruinart family: on 29 November 1821, Louis XVIII appointed him Mayor of Reims, taking over from the Baron Nicolas Ponsardin, who had died one year earlier. He was to remain at the head of the town's administration for nine years, until 1830.

The running of the town needed to be improved, and Irénée Ruinart got down to the job straight away. He set up a documentation committee responsible for putting order into the town's archives, which until then had been piled away haphazardly; he uncovered and restored the Roman triumphal arch that until then had been buried within the walls of the town—along which he planted Scotch firs. He was particularly concerned to improve the lot of workers and servants: so in 1822 he

Coat of arms granted by Louis XVIII to Irénée Ruinart de Brimont.

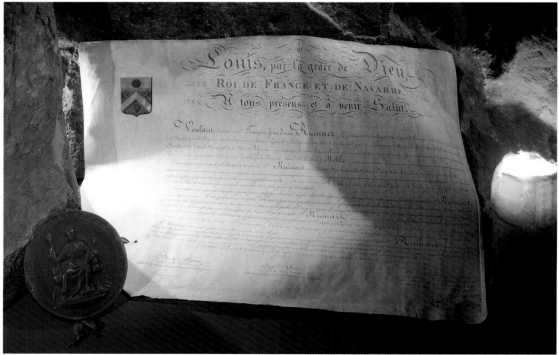

founded the municipal pawnshop, and, the next year, a savings and provident fund. And he was interested in the state of the public buildings of Reims. He therefore built the left wing of the town hall, which had remained in an unfinished state since 1606. And in 1824 he succeeded in persuading Charles X—whom he visited at the head of a delegation from Reims, to congratulate him on his accession to the throne—to promise a government grant to pay for repairs to the Archbishop's Palace, and—in contrast—to build new prisons. The royal promise was kept. All this activity added to his popularity and was doubtless a factor in his appointment, in 1823, as president of the electoral college of the 3rd *arrondissement* of the Marne; and he was again elected as Deputy. During this second mandate, he concerned himself particularly with the interests of the town of Reims, not forgetting that he was its most important public officer: so in 1825 he helped to obtain a municipal loan, and in 1826 gave his support to a petition by the craftsmen of Reims against smuggling. His activities as Deputy meant that he often stayed in Paris, where he bought lodgings in a *hôtel particulier* at 25 Rue Saint-Dominique, in the heart of the Faubourg Saint-Germain.

But let us return to 1825. Charles, previously Comte d'Artois, or simply "Monsieur", had become King of France a few months before. But he had not yet been solemnly confirmed by coronation as successor to Saint Louis. Although Louis XVIII had been glad to attend this ceremony, the new King had not yet taken any steps towards doing so. The leading citizens of Reims therefore went to Paris to ask him to come to be crowned in the ancient cathedral. The deputation was led by the Mayor, Irénée Ruinart de Brimont. Charles promised that he would come to Reims.

The following months were given over to intense preparations. Plans were drawn, buildings were repaired and smartened up, and arrangements were made to provide food and lodging for the royal family, their attendants, dignitaries and civil servants. Irénée Ruinart devoted himself entirely to this demanding task, giving orders, motivating the people working under him. Soon all was ready. The Mayor and his delegation returned to Paris to inform Charles X that Reims was expecting him.

On 28 May 1825, the eve of the coronation, the King arrived. Irénée Ruinart, at the head of the delegates from the town council, welcomed

"Plan for a savings and provident fund to be established in the town of Reims."
This document was submitted by the Vicomte Ruinart de Brimont to the Reims Chamber of Commerce.
Archives de la Marne.

him and presented him with the official gifts, with the words: "Sire, as one of our forebears said to Henri IV, so I will say to one of his descendants: we offer you the best of what we have—our wines, our pears, and our hearts. Please accept them."

He was referring to the pears from Rousselet that were famous throughout the region.

The next day, the King made his entrance into the town. His carriage stopped at the Porte de Vesle. There, the mayor was waiting for him, and, following the old custom, presented him with the keys of the town, before going to his seat in the cathedral, not far from his son, the Canon Albert Ruinart de Brimont, secretary to Monseigneur de Latil, the Archbishop of Reims. After the coronation, there were the celebrations, in which the whold town took part, and which lasted until 1 June. Irénée Ruinart was the constant companion of the King and the Duchesse de Berry, who granted an audience to Mme Ruinart and the Société des Dames de la Charité Maternelle de Reims. Nor did Irénée forget his responsibilities as Mayor: when he was in the town hall with the King, he pointed out that if an opening was made between the Place de la Ville and the Rue Royale, there would be a view as far as the Place Royale. The King promised to contribute funds towards the creation of a new street: this was to be the Rue Colbert, for which, in 1827, Ruinart sponsored the application to the Chamber of Deputies for a municipal loan.

He gave a banquet in his town house, the Hôtel de Joyeuse, in honour of his guest, the Duc de Clermont-Tonnerre, Minister of War. His grandson Thierry-Amédée describes this reception in a lively manuscript entitled *Memoirs of a Native of Reims*:

"A large banquet, to which members of the civil and military authorities were invited, was given in a marquee that had been put up in a magnificent avenue of chestnut trees in the garden. Dessert came in the shape of an enormous sugar helmet. I was hidden inside it, and when the butler opened up this monumental creation, I got out, very much alive, and to the great surprise of the guests. Even although I was very young at the time, I remember this strange detail, and also the white flag flying above the large entrance to the house, that had a canon on each side."

On 31 May, in order to thank him for his longstanding faithfulness to the Royalist cause, Charles X signed letters patent granting the title of viscount to Irénée Ruinart de Brimont. And on the same day, during a troop inspection near Reims, the King also made him an Officer of the Légion d'Honneur, and presented him with a diamond-studded gold snuffbox.

The Viscount Irénée Ruinart de Brimont was at the zenith of his career. The portrait of him by Germain—now hanging in the Château de Courtomer, the residence of his descendant the Comte de Pelet—dates back to this period. Copies of this portrait are to be found today in the town hall of Reims and at the headquarters of the Maison Ruinart, in the Rue des Crayères. He is shown in the dark blue, silver-embroidered uniform of an Officer of the Légion d'Honneur, and wears the medal of the Légion on his chest, with a white silk sash around his waist and a sword at his side. Symbolically, the town hall of Reims is shown in the background. There is a goose quill within reach. His face is full, his nose long and straight, and his chestnut hair is thick and wavy. He looks every bit a man of weight and distinction during the Restoration. No allusion is made in this portrait to his business. Champagne does not feature. There are no points in common with the pastel portrait, done about thirty years earlier, of his father Claude Ruinart, a busy merchant. This portrait in its heavy gilded frame announces loudly and clearly that socially, its subject has made it.

But Irénée Ruinart's political career was nearing its end. At a time when the forces of liberalism were making themselves increasingly felt, the government of Charles X was reactionary and conservative. In September 1829 the Chamber of Deputies was dissolved. Irénée was again president of the electoral college of Reims. But this time he was not re-elected: Jobert-Lucas, a liberal, was returned to the Chamber instead. It was a rude surprise for the newly-created Vicomte de Brimont, who, although not an *ultra*, was nevertheless a diehard conservative. In spite of the entreaties of a majority of the town's citizens, he resigned from his position as Mayor. And just as, eight years previously, Louis XVIII had appointed him to this office in order to make up for his first defeat in parliamentary elections, so Charles X now appointed him a Gentleman of the Royal Household by decree of 4 November 1829. But the monarchy did not have long to live, for the Bourbons were to fall the next year. In May 1830 the Chamber of Deputies was dissolved

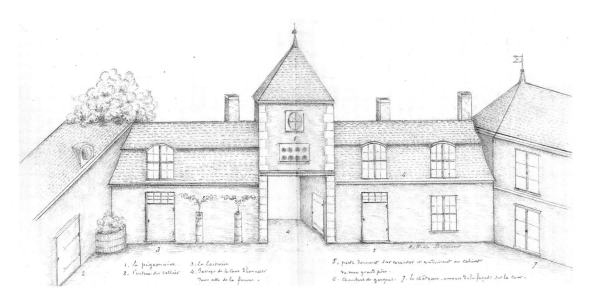

Drawing by Thierry-
Amédée Ruinart,
showing the inner
courtyard of the
Château de Brimont
as it was before its
destruction in the First
World War.
*Archives of the Comte
de Moulliac.*

for the second time. The electoral colleges were to return the new Deputies in July. And true to form, Irénée Ruinart was once again president of the electoral college of Reims. But it was no use: Jobert-Lucas, the outgoing Deputy, was re-elected. In Paris, the *ultra* government of the Duc de Polignac was foundering. The events surrounding the famous decrees of 27, 28 and 29 July 1830—the July Days—brought about its fall. The Parisians put up barricades in the streets and forced the last legitimate king to go into exile. The Duc d'Orléans—a client of the Maison Ruinart, incidentally—became Lieutenant-General of the kingdom, then pushed aside the young Duc de Bordeaux (future Comte de Chambord), grandson of Charles X, before ascending the throne as Louis-Philippe.

The King of France was no more, and had been replaced by the King of the French. There was a difference.

Like the vast majority of Legitimists, Irénée Ruinart de Brimont decided to retire from public life. From now until the end of his days he devoted his energies to charitable works, farming, and the study of economics.

He led an active retirement, continuing to work on various projects. In 1836 he and the *abbé* Charlier founded the Bethlehem Home for abandoned children, and he was also one of the founders of the Academy of Reims, as well as being an assiduous member of the Academy of Agriculture. And in 1839, shocked by the destitution in which certain

members of the Légion d'Honneur ended their days, he founded the Reims Association for Members of the Légion d'Honneur, one of the first of such associations, which were to spread throughout France.

Now a widower since 1835, he spent almost the whole year at Brimont. He rebuilt the *château*, which had been destroyed by fire in 1761. It was reached through a *cour d'honneur* on one side, and via a terrace and colonnade on the other. And there were two wings, an orangery, a greenhouse, and a gothic chapel, which all made for an imposing appearance. The grounds, laid out by a Reims horticulturist, included several ornamental ponds, a bridge in the rustic style, a hermit's house, and several ancient monuments found in the surrounding area. And since the owner was a famous wine-producer, a storeroom giving onto the *cour d'honneur* contained two wine presses and 2,500 casks of wine— all of which did not prevent Irénée Ruinart from producing honey and gruyère-style cheese, under the supervision of a Swissman and two assistants. Ruinart had become a real gentleman-farmer. His household consisted of a steward, a warden, and numerous servants.

Two drawings
showing the farm
workers' house, the
press-house, the
storeroom, and the
entry to the loft.
*Archives of the Comte
de Moulliac.*

Since he was rich, influential, and a touch paternalist, it was natural that he should arouse jealousy. It was this jealousy that had been at the root of his failure in the past to get himself elected as Deputy. But there was worse to come, for on 1 December 1828, a group of miscontents, spitefully claiming that Irénée had cornered the grain market, set fire to Brimont: the utmost exertions of the villagers and the Reims firemen were needed in order to put it out.

Irénée owned numerous properties, and was indeed one of the largest landowners in the *département*, with the second largest fortune in the Marne, after the Comte Roy, who was a *pair de France*. He possessed land in various places, including Berméricourt, Boult-sur-Suippes, Neufchâtel, Chouilly, Asfeld, most of the Forest of Montmort, the Château d'Orbais (sold "because of mosquitos"!), and, of course, Sillery, with its *château* and vineyards, which included the famous Clos de la Maréchale d'Estrées, producing one of the most renowned vintages of the whole of Champagne.

And that brings us back to champagne and the Maison Ruinart Père & Fils, which in the last pages has been

overshadowed by Irénée de Brimont's achievements in public life. Indeed, although he was a consummate wine expert and an exemplary manager of his business, his parliamentary and town hall duties allowed him to devote less and less time to it. There was nothing surprising in this—he could not be expected to do everything at the same time.

But he did not neglect the needs of his business. Until 1816, he ran it entirely by himself, and his wise decisions brought prosperity. Throughout the many difficulties caused first by the Empire's constant state of war and then by the Continental Blockade, he continued to believe fervently in the importance of maintaining and improving the quality of his wines. In 1813 he bought fifteen acres of vineyards at Aÿ, in one of the top wine-growing areas of Champagne. He was actively involved in selecting the growths, and always chose the best. And in the Montagne and the Vallée, he stopped buying the less sought-after wines, and determinedly bought only the best ones. He put quality first—a policy that his descendants were to pursue, and that is still pursued by the Maison Ruinart today.

It is he who must take the credit for the development of the English market. In spite of the political and economic obstacles, he persevered; and the English were soon to become Ruinart's most important customers. He maintained links with Russia, where some of his competitors were, however, to enjoy greater success. He had friends in St. Petersburg, such as the Baron de Roll, who mediated for him at various stages. But the Russian market was still a limited one that was to develop in later years.

During this period, every member of the family was involved in the business. Irénée, of course, but also his wife, his older brother Nicolas (before he retired), his mother, his uncle, the *abbé* Tronson du Coudray, who lived near Verdun, and, most importantly, various of his sons: Thierry, the oldest; Antoine, the second son, who was to be Vice-Consul in Moscow, then in Dublin; and lastly Edmond, his third son, who was to succeed him.

On 1 July 1816, Irénée decided to make two of his sons, Thierry and Edmond, partners in the family business. And so, in the presence of a *notaire* (roughly the equivalent of an English solicitor), he set up a company with a capital of 800,000 francs, of which he owned 650,000, Thierry owned 100,000, and Edmond owned 50,000. This partnership was intended to last for an initial period of five years; and then in 1821 Irénée extended it for a further five years, declaring that he thus wished "to give his two sons proof of his trust and affection". It is because of the existence of this family "commercial treaty" that we know that the Maison Ruinart Père & Fils was based not only in Reims (in Irénée's residence, the Hôtel de Joyeuse), but also at Brimont and at Aÿ, where there were cellars and storerooms. Mention is also made of the "London branch", which demonstrates the importance of the British market at that time. Each person's areas of responsibility are clearly defined:

"Monsieur Ruinart *père* will be responsible for general management and supervision; Monsieur Thierry Ruinart will deal mainly with everything concerning red wines and our business with French Flanders, the Kingdom of the Netherlands; Monsieur Edmond Ruinart will be responsible in particular for bottled wine, for correspondence with salesman abroad and bankers, for the investing of funds, for cash in hand, etc"

But this partnership, which was intended to be for a period of five years, was not to last that long.

NEXT PAGE
Portrait of Edmond Ruinart de Brimont (1795-1856).
Archives Ruinart, Reims.

BELOW

"In God's care and transported by Messrs Petit, Père & Fils....." A Ruinart Père & Fils bill of landing, dated 31 May 1828, for six crates of thirty-six bottles, made out to Mr. Epshaw in Bordeaux.
Archives Ruinart, Reims.

Mayor, Deputy and Viscount

Irénée wished to devote himself entirely to his parliamentary and town hall duties, and now, he said, wished to retire from business. On 1 July 1824, the partnership was thus wound up by common agreement.

Of course Irénée Ruinart de Brimont was to continue to take an interest in the ancestral family business—but from a distance. His sons carried on his work and the work of his predecessors. In order to guide them, he had written a short manual back in 1809, entitled *Advice and instructions given by Mr. Ruinart de Brimont to his sons Thierry and Edmond concerning the commerce of the wines of Champagne.* And in a few pages he gives them theoretical and practical advice based on his personal experience as well as on the accumulated experience of previous generations. There are detailed instructions concerning "A merchant's accounts", on exchange rates, on bills of landing, bills of exchange and consignment notes; and, in the second part, wise advice on "The selling of wine, and business voyages", as well as "Instructions for the preparation of red wines from Chapmagne".

The style throughout is elegant and dignified, and bears witness to not only to the author's grasp of historical perspectives, but also to his detailed knowledge of wine-growing and the champagne trade.

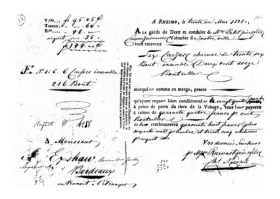

🍇 Irénée Ruinart de Brimont and Brigitte O'Garvey had nine children—a large

family, in keeping with the times, and whose various branches were, for the most part, to move away from the champagne trade, and, indeed, the Champagne area.

The oldest child, Claude Jean Thierry, normally known as Thierry, was born in 1791. We will return to him later, since along with his brother Jacques Edmond, four years his junior, he was, for a while, to have a hand in the destiny of the Maison Ruinart Père & Fils.

After Thierry there came three girls. The first two died at a young age; and in 1817, the third one, Marie, married M. Hériot de Vroël, a cavalry officer and the owner of the Château de Roquincourt, where she died eight years later, barely aged twenty-eight. Then came Antoine François, Vice-Consul in Hull, Moscow and Dublin, *chevalier* of the Légion d'Honneur, and who married Modeste Pelletier de Saint-Michel: for a very brief period he was to be involved in the family business, with just a small share in the partnership. Jacques Edmond, the third son, was to take over the management of the House of Ruinart. The fourth son, Jules-Albert, took up the ecclesiastical tradition of the family: ordained as a priest in 1826, he had a distinguished career. He was Vicar-General to the Cardinal de Latil, Archbishop of Reims, and the Pope sent him on several missions to the East; after which the Pope chose to make him a prelate, and he was appointed Canon of Saint Peter's in Rome. The eighth child, Jean Arthur, went into the Cour des Comptes (which monitors public expenditure) where he reached the rank of *conseiller-maître*; and in 1827 he married Laure de Chabrol-Chameane, who belonged to an influential family: her father was Deputy for la Nièvre, and a Gentleman of the King's Bedcamber, and her three uncles were Prefect of the Seine, Prefect of le Puy-de-Dôme, and Minister for the Navy. And finally, Irénée Ruinart's last son, Pierre-Henri, a Gentleman Ordinary of the King's Bedchamber, married Louise Boucher de Montuel, whose father was the Deputy for Orne. It was a fine family that the Mayor of Reims could be proud of.

Portrait of Antoine François Ruinart de Brimont (1793-1886), Vice-Consul. Collection of the Comte de Pelet, Château de Courtomer.

Nor was it surprising that things should turn out that way: success breeds success, and the Vicomte Irénée de Ruinart was nothing if not successful.

🐚 So in 1824, the two brothers Thierry and Edmond became joint controlling part-

ners of the business from which their father had decided to retire —although he was no doubt to remain a much-respected advisor. But Thierry, the oldest, did not aspire to play the same role as his father. He had previously studied under the *abbé* Liautard, whose renowned boarding school was to become the Collège Stanislas. Then, in spite of the Continental Blockade, his father sent him to England, where he learnt to speak English perfectly. Once back in Paris, he attended the Collège des Ecossais, in the Rue des Fossés-Saint-Victor. Right next door was the Dames-Anglaises (English Ladies) convent, whose mother superior was related to Mme Ruinart de Brimont. And amongst the boarders was Apolline Turgot, great niece of the famous Turgot. Her father was the Comte Antoine Turgot, Lieutenant-Colonel in command of the Place d'Oléron, and *chevalier de Saint-Louis*; and her grandfather, brother of Louis XVI's celebrated minister, had been Governor of Guyana.

The marriage took place in 1813, and Thierry's father gave him the property at Aÿ that he had just bought from M.de Loupeigne. The young man now found himself the owner of fifteen acres of vineyards on land at Aÿ, Mareuil-sur-Aÿ, Dizy, Montigny and Avernay, all producing champagne of *premier cru* quality: solid gold growing on vines. Thierry's father immediately started instructing him in the ways of business. He frequently travelled abroad, where, it seems, his straightforward but tactful manner was much appreciated.

Félicité de Lalot, second wife of Edmond Ruinart de Brimont. Oil on canvas. *Archives Ruinart, Reims.*

For reasons that we do not know—but that must have been related to the differences in character between the two brothers, which increasingly gave rise to disagreements—the partnership between Thierry and his brother Edmond, entered into in 1824, did not last long: for on 17 February 1826 Thierry ceded his share in the partnership to Edmond, who was to "continue the business alone", to quote the words of the transfer contract signed on 1 July to confirm the arrangement. And the two brothers agreed that in the event of further disagreements they would submit matters to their father's arbitration.

For a rew more years Thierry Ruinart de Brimont stayed in Reims, where he lived in the Hôtel de Joyeuse in the Place de la Ville. Then, concerned for the education of his ten children, he left for Paris in 1833, and sold his *hôtel* to his brother Edmond, keeping only the property at Aÿ, and even that for a short time.

Edmond Ruinart de Brimont was now therefore the sole master of the Maison Ruinart Père & Fils. Left a widower by the death of his wife Marie-Caroline Paté de Vandière, who died in 1819, after barely two years of marriage, he got married a second time, to Félicité de Lalot, whose father was a Deputy.

What state of affairs did he find? The French economy was not flourishing, and business was difficult. But from 1829 onwards, and during the July Monarchy, the situation improved, especially for the wine trade, which, to quote M. Decrock, "started to become a full-scale industry, with new chapmagne producers continually entering the market". "Make money", said Guizot: and businessmen followed his advice. And now, in these changing circumstances, the Maison Ruinart Père & Fils even began, for the first time, to sell its produce to other producers, mainly to Heidsieck and to Roederer.

In France, the clientèle was still made up mainly of restaurants, drinking establishments, and wine-merchants, especially in Bordeaux. And, as a sign of the times, financiers and stockbrokers figured particularly prominently. High Society still bought from Ruinart: clients included various *pairs de France*, ambassadors (the Prussian one, for example), aristocrats, and also churchmen, such as Monseigneur Garibaldi, the Vatican's *chargé d'affaires*.

Like his father, Edmond Ruinart believed in exporting. And in any case, several regional markets in France were stagnant, such as Lorraine, the Vosges, and Normandy. The Maison Ruinart continued to devoted as much energy as before to abroad, with good results. Sales were buoyant in Belgium (mainly in Brussels) and also in Holland (The Hague, Amsterdam and Rotterdam). But Edmond was more ambitious than that. He went to Russia. In 1827, a passport—now in the Ruinart archives—was issued by the Imperial Russian government. Signed by Count Nesselrode, Foreign Minister of Tsar Nicholas I, it simply states that M. Ruinart de Brimont is authorised to travel in Russia. We do not know the circumstances surrounding the long journey, or the results that it brought. From now on Russia was a small but steady market.

Between 1840 and 1850, most of Ruinart's sales in Russia were in St. Petersburg and Moscow. The clients were often shops and merchants, for example Depret & Fils in Moscow, and Eliseev, the famous delicatessen in Nevsky Prospect in St. Petersburg, suppliers to the city's most distinguished inhabitants. There were the Maison Ruinart's non-trade clients—English, Germans and Italians, doubtless diplomats: Lord Bloomfield, Sir Hamilton Seymour, Lord Stuart de Rothesay, the Cavaliere Ruffo di Castelcicala, the Baron von Plessen. And then there were clients amongst the Russian aristocracy: Prince Boris Galitzine, Count Leon Kotchoubey, and Mr. Kakevsky. Finally, in 1842 and 1846, large quantities of Ruinart champagne were delivered to the Grand Duke Michael, brother of the Tsar himself.

Edmond Ruinart de Brimont, at the time of his journey to Russia, and shortly before he went to the Uunited States. Original drawing by C. Blaize, 1827. Archives Ruinart, Reims.

But Edmond Ruinart had grand hopes for another country: the United States. In 1831, he made up his mind to go and seek out business in person in this new market that was of increasing importance to Europe. At that time, a voyage across the Atlantic was no small undertaking: "Since my business with the United States had been greatly increasing over the previous years, I conceived the plan of undertaking this long journey, especially since I was conscious of the importance of establishing more solid relations there, rather than basing my actions on vague and unreliable information picked up by chance and through hearsay —information that always carried a residue of doubt and uncertainty. I had to change this unsatisfactory state of affairs, otherwise I would fail to fully exploit a market that looked most promising. I will go further: ordinary good sense obliged me to abandon this way of doing business, unless I could make it more reliable—and how could I do that by letter? I had already exhausted several expedients. I saw around me the success of my competitors in this market. I was prompted by a natural pride to seek to preserve the standing of my business..."

These are the strong-willed opening words of a valuable book, the *Journal of a Voyage to America*, in which Edmond Ruinart wrote his impressions every day. We still have the manuscript. The head of the Maison Ruinart Père & Fils filled several dozen pages with his small and elegant handwriting. But surprisingly, this *Journal* records the voyage from the anecdotal point of view of a tourist. With few exceptions, there is no mention of his business or commercial activity. On the other hand, the book is full of descriptions of scenery, and portraits of people and customs. Although the *Journal* shows how important his travels in America were to the author, it sadly throws no light on the affairs of the Maison Ruinart. Here are a few passages which show the author's vigorous style, and which have an anecdotal interest of their own:

"My wife, my father, my mother—in short, all those who were dearest to me, discouraged me from going ahead with my plan, but I was not to be dissuaded, especially since I had recently received news from America that further illustrated the necessity of taking active steps to set my business in a new direction."

After he had arranged for the running of his affairs during his absence, he left Reims at the beginning of May 1831, spent several days with his family in Paris, and then—carrying letters of credit and letters of recommendation from his bankers, Hottinguer, Pereire, and Laffite: the great banking names of Paris at that time—he left for Le Havre. There, he embarked on the *Henri IV*, a four hundred and fifty-ton ship with three masts, commanded by Captain Cartoff: "One of the youngest captains of the line of ships, not yet being forty... He owed his position to his intelligence and seafaring knowledge. He had started his career at sea at an early age, as ship's boy. I cannot bring myself to praise his manners, since he was a true sea-dog, unsociable, and smoked over twenty cigars a day; we could not hope to spend time enjoyably in his society..." The "we" refers to Edmond's travelling companions: an Englishman, an Irishman ("frequently arguing over politics"), and a businessman from Paris. In the rear-deck there were one hundred and sixty-seven emigrants who were leaving Switzerland, Germany, and Alsace for the New World. After "a cow, some pigs and fowl" had been embarked, the *Henri IV* set sail on the morning of 18 May. The crossing lasted for thirty-eight days, and was enlivened by various incidents, cheerful and less cheerful, but on the whole of no great note. On 11 June, Edmond Ruinart spotted some icebergs: "vast bulks floating in the ocean and that had come from the North Pole."

Near Newfoundland, there were sightings of more icebergs, and of whales, one of which "came close to the boat". And soon after, they encountered some sharks, that Edmond was sad not to be able to harpoon.

Portrait, presumed to be of Caroline de Vardière, first wife of Edmond Ruinart de Brimont.
Oil on canvas.
Archives Ruinart, Reims.

And finally, on 24 June, the ship entered the harbour of New York; and almost ran aground, due a mistake on the part of the captain, put right in time by the pilot who came out from the port.

As soon as he was ashore and settled in the Marion House Hotel, the traveller met several French friends and business colleagues, and even Ruinart's Amsterdam agent.

He then set to work, "intending to return to France in October, in time for the grape harvest". In his *Journal*, he gives a detailed description of Broadway, New York's business district, near the quays, comparing it to the City of London. "A big street four or five miles long, crossing the town in a straight line... with streets running parallel through a respectable area". His description—as good as a guidebook—is accompanied by comments on trade and the economy in America. After a three-week stay in New York, he left for Philadelphia, Baltimore, and Washington. He travelled partly by steamboat, whose paddle wheels thrashed the water in keeping with the best traditions of the West of America, and partly by railway, an extraordinary novelty that did not, however, seem to impress him excessively. "The carriages, of which there were twenty, held about 300 people, and were pulled by a steam engine. This procession struck me as being most bizarre; and considering the speed at which we were travelling—roughly between 6 and 8 leagues an hour—I did not feel very safe, especially since to one side of me there was a precipice with the waters of the Patapsco at the bottom..."

Near Baltimore, he spent two days at Doneghen Manor, belonging to his friend Caroll, grandson of a Senator, and "one of the richest landowners in the United States". His comment on slavery is as follows: "The slaves' village is a quarter of a league from his residence. There are about 300 or 400 of them... These slaves are very happy, since their master is kind and fair, but this is not always the case elsewhere, espe-

Passport issued on 11 November 1825 by the Prefect of the Marne to Jean Thierry Ruinart, "eldest son, landowner", allowing him to travel "to London and other cities of the Kingdom of Great Britain", on business for the Maison Ruinart. This passport, bearing the royal arms, is signed on the back by "the *chevalier* Ruinart de Brimont", French Vice-Consul in Hull, and dated 3 January 1826, "to return to France".
The signature belongs to Thierry's younger brother, Antoine François.
Archives Ruinart, Reims.

cially in the southern States. Many masters treat them cruelly. A fine young specimen of a male slave is worth between 450 and 500 dollars... These people, apart from farming the land, are trained in a skill, so that their master has masons, locksmiths and carpenters to hand."

In Baltimore, he stayed in "an enormous hotel, the biggest in the United States, called Barnum's Hotel. It has 200 beds, several vast reception rooms, and is situated in one of the best areas of the town". Finally, he left for Washington, determined to meet the President of the United States. Thanks to an introduction to Mr. Donaldson, the President's secretary, he succeeded in being introduced to General Jackson during an assembly at the Capitol, whose architecture and general appearance much impressed him.

"As [Donaldson] knew... that I most keenly desired to be introduced to the President, he asked me to follow him, saying that he would take me to him straight away, even though there were already surrounded by several people. On going into the large reception room, I saw an old man with tied back white hair, tall and thin, smoking a pipe, and nearby several people seated and talking to him. Mr. Donaldson introduced me to the General, who stood up and took my hand, inviting me to sit down. He then introduced me, in English, to the other people there, as is the custom in America, and they carried on with their conversation... After a while, the President asked me several questions about France, and concluded our conversation by saying that he hoped that in a year's time our government [under Louis-Philippe] would be firmly established and free from further upheavals. Since the President had been unwell due to a tour of the States that he had just completed, I congratulated him on his recovery, and then took leave of him after he had shaken me by the hand.

As can be imagined, this encounter left an impression, and I was most pleased and flattered by the reception that had been given to me, and struck by the simple manners of the President, head of this immense republic, calmly smoking his pipe like an old veteran...."

Unfortunately, Edmond Ruinart's *Journal* ends not long after this visit, so we do not know anything about the last stages of his voyage, which ended several days later. Nor does the Journal leave us any the wiser about the commercial aspects of this expedition. But lastly, let us look at a passage, full of flavour, concerning the American character:

"I must observe... that the Americans are extremely enterprising. Nothing frightens them. They even seek out difficulties so that they can enjoy the credit of overcoming them; so everywhere, one sees works of the greatest skill, that nobody in Europe would dare to undertake. It is true that there are lots of accidents, and one frequently hears of people who have been killed or crushed by falling objects, by steam-boats exploding, by shipwrecks, etc. Almost every day the newspapers carry stories of foolhardiness or accidents. But in spite of this, nobody thinks of taking precautions, and the national attitude is "We must go along". And on this front they cannot be reproached."

Claude Jean Thierry Ruinart de Brimont photographed at Versailles towards the end of his life. *Archives of the Comte de Mouliac.*

❧ There is very little information about the period that followed the return from America. We only know that in 1833 Edmond Ruinart de Brimont bought the *hôtel* in the Place de la Ville from his brother Thierry, who was now firmly established in Paris in a *hôtel particulier* in Rue Cassette. And it as also in Paris that Elisabeth Ruinart de Brimont, wife of Irénée and mother of Edmond, died on 13 May 1835. She did not live long enough to witness the quarrel between her sons: for in 1837 a nasty disagreement arose between the two brothers. Edmond accused Thierry of taking "a few profits on the side" by selling some wine to some friends at the end of an arrangement made during the period when Thierry handed over control of the Maison Ruinart to his younger brother. It is difficult to see why the issue mattered so much. But Edmond became angry, and claimed that his brother was running the business in a way that failed to respect the agreements that they had entered into in 1826. It seems that he got carried away and started legal proceedings. The dispute ended up in court, in an ugly trial in Reims, with a judge's ruling (at the request of their father Irénée) that went against Thierry, who was represented by the great lawyer Berryer, counsel for the defence to the Duchesse de Berry. The choice of this advocate says a great deal about the the Legitimist opinions of the Ruinart family. And a few years later, in 1848, Thierry sold the property at Aÿ and its vineyards to M. Moët, of Épernay—a loss that his descendants were to deplore, but which is surely an indication of the considerable bitterness he felt.

From now on, the family's only really exceptional vineyards were those at Sillery. Nor did broader circumstances favour the family. In France, the Revolution of 1848 brought about the fall of the July Monarchy, and the coming to power of Louis-Napoleon Bonaparte, *Prince-Président*, and then Emperor from 1851. The Ruinart family's well-known Legitimist opinions excluded them from favour under the Second Empire. These opinions are clearly expressed in an unpublished manuscript entitled *Memoirs of an Native of Reims*, written by Amédée Ruinart de Brimont, whom we have already come across several times. Son of Thierry (Edmond's brother), and a lively writer with a charming style, he recounts his life in the capital and elsewhere, and gives a particularly vivid description of the Revolution of 1848, which he saw as an officer in the National Guard. The following passage clearly suggests how the Ruinart family felt at the time:

"Lots of families that had pledged allegiance to the senior branch [of the Bourbons] had subsequently rallied to Louis-Philippe. My family had remained amongst those who refused to compromise their principles, and since this was well-known in high places, we were kept out of all the positions of influence to which our abilities and education should have given us access..."

Thierry Amédée Ruinart de Brimont (1823-1904). Grandson of Irénée, and Sub-Prefect of Cosne-sur-Loire (Nièvre), he was the historiographer of his family and left behind him several manuscripts full of information and reminiscences. *Archives of the Comte de Mouillac, his great-grandson.*

The Second Empire, now just beginning, opened a period of partying and festivities that necessarily involved champagne. All the same, it seems that to begin with, the Maison Ruinart Père & Fils did not benefit much from all this.

On 4 January 1850, the Vicomte Irénée, patriarch of the family, died in Reims. He had divided his wealth amongst his children, and had left numerous generous legacies, especially to the poor. His will was an model of highmindedness, an example to his family. But they no longer got on well together, and they argued in an ugly way over their father's inheritance. The family of Thierry Ruinart de Brimont, the oldest son, now living entirely in Paris, were never to forget the

The Conquest of the New World

experience. In particular, the Château de Brimont, which should have gone to Thierry, went to his younger brother Henri, who died there in 1868.

Abroad, the Belgian and Dutch markets were hardly vigorous. The German states were buying much less, with one notable exception: Bavaria, where the sovereigns (the country had become a kingdom in 1805), the Court, and the capital, Munich, were buying considerable quantities of Ruinart champagne. Next came Berlin, and the ports of Hamburg and Bremen. Russia, with whom diplomatic relations became tense in the period leading up to the Crimean War, completely stopped buying from 1854; and that market was not to open up for several years. Although Edmond Ruinart de Brimont, at under sixty, was young, he tired of the business. According to his nephew Amédée, he had become silent, sour, terse, and difficult to be with. And like his father and grandfather before him, he decided to retire. In 1854, he left the Maison Ruinart to Charles and Edgar, his two sons by his second wife Félicité de Lalot. He did not enjoy his retirement long, since he died two years later, on 28 January 1856, at the end of a drawn-out period of agony. A macabre event accompanied his death: his wife, keen to be at his bedside, broke a leg and was unable to be with him in his last moments. She did not recover from this accident, and died several months later, on 22 April.

So now a new generation of the family took charge of the Maison Ruinart: a generation that was to continue the tradition of exporting, discovering new markets for champagne.

Edgar (1829-1881) and Charles (1824-1896)
Ruinart de Brimont:
from the Bubbles of the Second Empire
to the Bubbles of the Third Republic

❦ For the third time
in three generations, two brothers took over from their

father. There were five years between Charles and Edgar Ruinart de Brimont—the former was born in 1824, and the latter in 1829. They started by learning the business alongside their father, and took sole control in 1854. But Charles very soon left the Maison Ruinart, which was thereafter in the hands of his younger brother, aged only just thirty. France was at that time living at the hectic pace of the Second Empire. Napoleon III was reigning at the Tuileries. The epoch is associated with the operettas of Offenbach, whose light and carefree music captured Paris and Vienna. The Court danced lightheaded to the waltzes of Strauss. Offenbach was himself a client of the Maison Ruinart from 1857: it is easy to imagine him drinking their champagne as he composed *La Vie Parisienne*, *La Grande Duchesse de Geroldstein*, or *La Belle Hélène*. And if Ruinart champagne was good for drinking, it was good for dancing too—the composer Arban wrote the *Ruinart Polka*, which he dedicated to Edgar. There were other distinguished names of the Second Empire who drank the champagne from the Rue des Crayères: the Comte de La Rochefoucauld; the Baron Janes de Rothschild, celebrated banker, owner of the Château de Ferrières, and friend of Napoleon III and the Empress Eugenie; the Princesse de Solms; Edmond About, the famous dramatic writer and composer; and the Comtesse de Laubespin. And Ruinart champagne was delivered to clients in the Army: Colonel the Comte Pajol, General the Marquis de Gronchy, and also the officers' mess of

Charles Ruinart de Brimont (1824-1896). *Archives Ruinart, Reims.*

the 1st Cavalry of the Imperial Guard. Indeed, various members of the Ruinart de Brimont family not close enough to the senior branch to be involved in the business, went into the Army, which was a fashionable career under Napoleon III. And so four sons of the Vicomte Thierry —Rémi, Pierre, Paul and Xavier, all, of course, cousins of the head of the Maison Ruinart—served as officers in the Lancers and in the *Chasseurs d'Afrique* (a light cavalry regiment). Pierre was killed in 1859 at the Battle of Solférino, in which his twin-brother Paul fought: he resigned his commission soon after. But this prestigious clientèle, which included restaurants, cafés and various wholesalers—all a regular source of business—was only part of the picture, since in good years and bad, only 10 to 16% of the Maison Ruinart's sales were made in France. This proportion, which held good until about 1860, was, if anything, tending to fall off. All the same, for the first time in its history, Ruinart started to sell champagne in the south-west of France, in Carcassonne, Pau, Orthez, and especially Toulouse. As before, most of their business was done abroad: in this sense, the commercial strategy of the Maison Ruinart remained unchanged.

Abroad, but where exactly? The development of Ruinart's market depended not only on the results of business voyages, but also on politics. And so exports to Italy and Austria disappeared in the wake of the war in 1859 between these countries and France; although there was one exception—a delivery, in December 1860, to Cardinal Mattei in Rome. The German market was much weaker, with 16% of total sales, against 28% at the beginning of the century. Only Frankfurt, Mayence, and Stuttgart were buying more than before. But there nevertheless remained a sizeable and prestigious clientèle. There are entries in the book for the Duke of Brunswick (between 1856 and 1861), the Grand Duke of Oldenburg (1857-1859), and even a certain von Bismark in Külz. The main German client, however, was Bavaria, faithful as ever. The royal Court was at the top of the list, followed by the Princes Karl and Luitpold of Bavaria, uncles (or brothers) of Ludwig II, owner of castles, patron of Wagner, and fervent drinker of champagne. And then there was the Prince Clodwig of Hohenlohe-Schillingsfurst, Prime Minister of Bavaria in 1866; and also Prince Charles of Oettingen-Wallerstein.

Belgium also remained faithful to Ruinart, with almost 21% of total sales. The most important client was King Leopold I, to whom orders were sent regularly. Among other regular clients were the Prince de Chimay in Brussels, the Comte de Mercy-Argenteau in Liège, Mme de Biolley at Beviers, the Baronne de Chambronne in Tournau, and the Comte Charles d'Oultremont at the Château de Presle. Ypres, Courtrai and Liège were a good market, with Liège neck and neck with Brussels, or even ahead.

Northern Europe—Holland and Scandinavia—accounted for only about 1% of Ruinart's sales, and was a market that had been declining since

Order from the Queen Mother of Bavaria, dated 9 May 1865, to be paid for via Mallet Frères & Compagnie, a bank in Paris. The order is signed by the Count von Pappenheim. *Archives Ruinart, Reims.*

the eighteenth century. The only client there who features in the books is Sir Andrew Buchanan, His Britannic Majesty's Minister Plenipotentiary in Copenhagen. Spain is in the books simply for the sake of putting in an appearance (0.3% of total sales in 1859), and in spite of Edmond Ruinart's business voyage in 1831, the United States still accounted for under 1% (0.9% in 1871).

Ruinart's largest market—and it had only recently become important—was now England. The instability of the relations between France and England had created unpredictable ups and downs in Ruinart's sales across the Channel, but demand there was buoyant in the second half of the century. The main reason for this was the commercial treaty of January 1860 between Napoleon III and Queen Victoria, continuing the spirit of the famous *Entente Cordiale* inaugurated by the Queen and Louis-Philippe, King of the French. This teaty, which completed the process of liberalisation that marked the Second Empire, considerably lowered the customs duties beteen the two countries; and in the treaty, England also gave favourable customs treatment to imports of wine and certain luxury products. For two generations the Maison Ruinart had in any case been very well disposed towards England, and they now consolidated their position, with the help of their London representative, "John Ruinart" [?] of 8 Leicester Square, then 22 St Swithin's Lane, in the City. Sales in the British market increased: from two fifths of total sales in 1860, to more that three quarters twenty-five years later. In the second half of the nineteenth century, this was therefore by far the most important of Ruinart's markets. Most of the sales were made in London, followed by Dublin, Newcastle, Liverpool,

Advertisement for Whitlock Nichols & Co, Ruinart's New York agents. Archives Ruinart, Reims.

Edinburgh and Glasgow; and champagne was also popular in Scotland, where whisky was less fashionable than now. Ruinart sold champagne not only in England, but also in the British Empire: in Malta, and in India, especialy in Bengal, Shansi, Sealki—garrison towns where the British officers had a liking for Ruinart—and also Calcutta, now easier to reach after the opening of the Suez Canal in 1869.

A Ruinart *collerette*, bearing the words "Suppliers to the Court of His Majesty the King of Bavaria." *Archives Ruinart, Reims.*

🍇 Russia, whose frontiers had of course been closed to France during the

Crimean War (1854-1855), continued to interest Ruinart Père & Fils. The Tsar Alexander II, who abolished serfdom in 1856, was moderately francophile. His visit to Paris, in 1867, was to be marked by an assassination attempt by a Polish nationalist.

Just as his father had been interested in the United States, Edgar Ruinart de Brimont was interested in the Russian Empire. So in 1859, almost thirty years after his father's voyage, he undertook a similar voyage to Russia. And like his father, he kept a journal, but shorter and less detailed: notes jotted down rapidly, as ideas occurred to him, and almost entirely without descriptions or general reflections. Strangely, the journal is written in English throughout, with only the occasional sentence or expression in French.

He left Reims on 9 December 1859, with his wife, an Englishwoman called Mina Sheppard, and also a Miss Crampton, doubtless one of Mme de Brimont's maids; they travelled with him as far as Paris. Then, accompanied only by a certain Grognet, probably his secretary, he went, via Berlin, to Koenigsberg. And there, he engaged a German valet, the young Frederick, "an intelligent young devil", who, for a salary of 85 thalers a month, was to accompany him during his travels—which turned out to be more difficult than those of his father in America. They travelled by coach drawn by four horses, and then by sledge: the horses had to be changed at the post houses, and Edgar Ruinart carried a letter to be sure of being given the best ones as promptly as possible. They crossed the boarder with Russia on 17 December, in the company of a certain Princess T., "a very pretty and elegant young lady". The traveller was horrified to see old soldiers dressed in rags. He was attracted by another young princess, beautiful and lively, wife of a Frenchman called Duloup, with whom he did not get on well, and who seemed to be jealous of him. Ruinart was so worried that he "kept his postols ready". The cold was intense, and the snow thick, and Ruinart suffered from pains in one leg and a sore throat, and complained that he could not smoke. The travellers would willingly have swapped their post horses for a train, but the railway network was in its initial stages of development, and had not reached that part of the country. And in a post house near Dunaburg, they even had to give two bottles of Ruinart to a groom in order to get fresh horses. They continued their journey in "appaling" conditions. Grognet said that he had not seen so much snow for twelve years. The sledge was pulled by five horses and driven by two postilions. Edgar Ruinart's opinion of the Russians was coloured by the situation: "The educated classes have a veneer of culture. They talk about everything, but know nothing, speak several languages, and drink enormous quantities"—which should after all have pleased a wine merchant. As for the peasants, "They would as soon kill a man as drink a cup of tea. The poor are poorer than can be imagined. The soldiers are at the bottom of the pile. There are no pensions and no hospitals for old people." These were biting comments, based on a limited and biased experience of the country, which was certainly less developed than the West, but which did all the same have a minimum level of social structures. Doubtless worn out by the hardships of the journey, Ruinart went so far as to say that intelligence was unknown in Russia, and that the inhabitants were "anything but civilised". Why on earth had he got involved in this journey? To make matters worse, the sleigh ran against a stone, and ended up on its side in the snow. Grognet got angry, and "hit everyone". After eighteen hours of journey by sleigh, the travellers arrived at Ostrov. In spite of some "good soup" and an attractive room, Ruinart wrote: "I have never been so miserable in my life." On the road again the next day, the sight of sleighs in "three feet of snow" made him think of "our army in 1815" (he meant 1812). Finally the travellers—they were still with the Duloups—reached Pskov, where they stayed in the Hôtel de Paris, before reaching St. Petersburg on 23 December 1861. Still suffering from pains in one leg, and with a headache too, he eventually managed to find a room on the third floor of the Hôtel de Paris (Again! The French capital obviously had a good reputation!).

Edgar Ruinart de Brimont (1829-1881). After his father's journey to the United States, he left for Russia in 1861. *Archives Ruinart, Reims.*

The next day, he visited the French Embassy ("splendid") and met the Comte Gaston de Montebello, for the time being just an *attaché*, but later to be French Ambassador. On Saturday he had to report to the young Count Chouvalov, Minister of Police, "almost too friendly, clearly a Russian just like the rest of them" (nothing made him happy), who said that he had "opened a good many bottles of Ruinart in his time". The only reaction to this profession of faith was the comment: "He'll be useful..."!

Then he got down to work, which notably involved visiting various English business-men, like Thomson Bonar, who had establi-shed themselves as representatives in Russia of producers of spirits; and he visited a certain Schultz, a German. Edgar Ruinart was also given a warm reception by Robert Colqhoon, editor of the *English Magazine*, who was to serve as mentor to him throughout his visit. "My English has never been so useful," he wrote in his journal. Schultz also introduced him to various British and German wine bro-kers. The evenings were given over to amu-sements and socialising. There was the opera, where he heard the famous soprano Rosati —"an adorable creature, but none too

Eliseev, the enormous delicatessen on Nevsky Prospect in St. Petersburg. Ruinart champagne was on sale there. Collection of Patrick de Gmeline.

pretty"—and saw her talking to the Tsar himself; and the French soprano Mangin, now living in Russia in great style. And there were diners in the famous St. Petersburg restaurants Petit and Dupont, whose names and chefs were decidedly French, and which were full of officers drinking champagne—Moët! He dined with a certain Nauer, half Russian, whose father had met his own father thirty years pre-viously: confirmation of a voyage to Russia in 1827 about which we know almost nothing. He also dined with the Duke of Ossuna, and met the Count Laval, a Russian aristocrat of French origin, and a member of the Jockey Club; and was invited by General Cotte, Equerry of the Tsar, to visit the Imperial stables.

On 1 January 1860 he wrote that he would have to play "doubles or quits", doubtless a reference to his commercial relations with Russia; but he was afraid that his physical condition (his leg was still hurting) would prevent him from making the most of this visit.

"If I do not succeed—he wrote—I will not regret this journey, which is undertaken in the best interests of the Maison Ruinart. And if the effort and hardships of this journey are to be rewarded in just proportion, my success will be great indeed." It is not clear whether he was thinking of the contract signed with Schultz, whose contents we do not know.

Shortly before leaving St. Petersburg, he met the famous Eliseev, owner of the delicatessen in Nevsky Prospect: "squat and dirty", but eloquent on the subject of the Maison Ruinart, having sold 2,000 of their bottles the year before. Edgar drank tea with him, and thought that he was being poisoned, no doubt by the dirtiness.

A small detail: in his journal, Edgar refers to his champagne as "bottles of R.", foreshadowing a development that was to come a century later, when the *cuvée* called R was to be at the heart of the Maison Ruinart's range.

On 5 January, he left by train for Moscow. For once he was comfortable; and found himself in the company of an amiable gentleman who was addressed as "General", but whom he did not think much of, and suspected of being an adventurer. After a full twenty-three hours in the train, he arrived in Moscow, where it was snowing, and settled into the Russia Hotel. He could not use his interpreter, a certain Alexander, to whom he had given ten bottles of Ruinart the evening before, and who was later found dead drunk. The visit to Moscow does not seem to have pleased Edgar as much as the one to St. Petersburg, in spite of the help of Dupret, his permanent representative there. Dupret told him, strangely, that champagne was crashing in Russia; and was astonished to hear of the craze for it in St. Petersburg. After visiting the Kremlin, which he found "very curious, especially the rooms of the maids of honour", he returned to St. Petersburg and spent a week there before leaving for France. He travelled first by train, then by sledge, which he shared with a certain M. de Château-Renaud, a diplomat returning to his posting in London, and with whom he immediately got on well. On 20 January, the travellers arrived in Cologne, and Edgar telegraphed his wife Mina to say that he was on his way to Reims. The voyage to Russia was over.

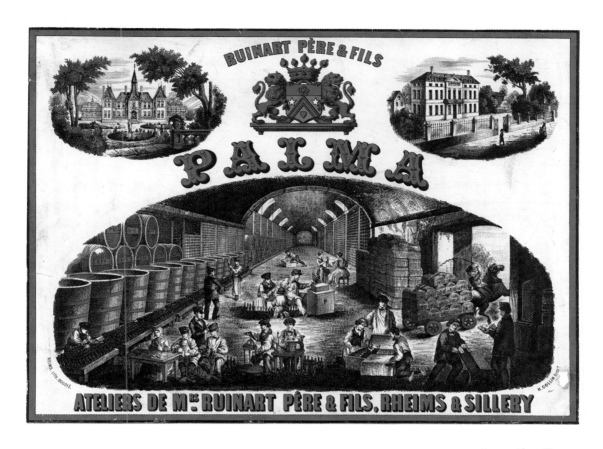

Sales certainly benefited from Edgar's journey. But the Russian market towards the close of the nineteenth century was not at any stage of great importance for the Maison Ruinart.

🍇 In 1870 war broke out between Prussia and France.

Within a few weeks, Napoleon III was beaten and an armistice was signed at Sedan: the town had fallen, together with the army and the Emperor. Amongst the French prisoners was Thierry's last son, Xavier Ruinart de Brimont, a Captain in the *Chasseurs d'Afrique*. He was set free not long after, and subsequently left for Algeria, where he died at Blinda in 1876.

France was now occupied, and the Prussians entered Reims on 4 September 1870. Wilhelm I, King of Prussia and soon to be Emperor of

Germany, visited the town on the 5th, accompanied by Chancellor Bismark and General von Moltke. In Paris, revolution broke out and swept away the Second Empire, which was replaced by the Commune, while the enemy watched from outside the city walls.

In Reims, economic activity came to a halt; and with it, for several months, Ruinart's sales. No record exists in their books of business done in France between 3 August 1870 and 12 April 1871. Edgar Ruinart, Mayor of Sillery, saw no reason for undue stubbornness, and for the time being left for calmer surroundings. But he came back before long.

The Prussians occupied Reims. They were accompanied by their allies the Bavarians, old clients of the Maison Ruinart. From October 1870 onwards, officers' messes—especially that of the 16th Dragoons—demanded champagne from the famous producers, Ruinart among them. A certain Colonel Riese was in charge of purchases, and the champagne producers could choose between him or requisition—in other words, theft. Sales picked up bit by bit. Obviously the French market suffered from the war. The French had neither the inclination nor the money to buy champagne. The enormous war indemnity imposed by the victorious invaders caused a terrible economic crisis that affected all sectors.

Exports to Germany recovered, and to Bavaria, to Mayence, Stuttgart, Nuremberg and Munich, and also to Austria and Vienna; even if in quantities of a dozen or a half-dozen bottles, or sometimes fewer. In fact the Viennese market, which had for so long set the trend for the other German markets, was in sharp decline.

Sales also picked up in the Belgian market, which had not been affected by the war and to which French trains had free access; but the quantities were smaller than before. Nor did the new King, Leopold II, who acceded to the throne in 1865, seem to have the same taste for champagne as his predecessor: he stopped buying it after the Franco-Prussian War. Nevertheless, on 9 June 1874, Ruinart Père & Fils became "Suppliers to the Court of His Majesty the King of the Belgians"—the first event of its kind. This honour—whose commercial benefits for Ruinart were not negligible, even outside Belgium—resulted from negotiations carried out by the Baron d'Anethan on behalf of Edgar Ruinart de Brimont. The good news reached Reims in an official communication from the King's Cabinet bearing the signature of the Comte Paul de Borchgrave, the King's secretary.

In spite of having come to an almost complete halt between September 1870 and January 1871, exports to England picked up as soon as the situation became normal—if Prussian occupation of France can be called normal.

And lastly, the only noteworthy commercial event of this period was the export to San Francisco of 1,800 bottles of Ruinart via the agency of the wine brokers Macfarlane, Blair & Co. It was the first big sale in the United States, and was an important event that marked the opening up of the American market.

Over the next ten years, already-established trends were consolidated. The Pyrenean market—including Spain—stagnated. Austria was no longer buying, and apart from Bavaria, the German market was much weaker: Edmond Ruinart did not benefit from the dynamism of the young German Empire. On the other hand, England not only remained an important client, but became more important still, buying 84% of the Maison Ruinart's total sales. Such a concentration of sales in one market was not without its dangers.

Detail from a label.
Archives Ruinart, Reims.

✿ Like his predecessors,
Edgar Ruinart de Brimont did not compromise on

the quality of the wines from which he made his champagne. The books for 1861 show that 42% of his purchases came from various vineyards in the Vallée: Aÿ, Dizy, Hautvillers, Damery, Épernay and Saint-Martin d'Abbois. A further 32% came from the Côte des Blancs: Mesnil, Vertus, and Cramant. And 26% came from the Montagne de Reims: Bouzy, Ambonnay, Mailly and Verzenay. They were all *grands crus*, and could only enhance the image and taste of Ruinart champagne. Unlike at the beginning of the century, there is no sign in the books of the wines from the Saint Thierry massif, or from Bordeaux and Burgundy—these had now been replaced largely by the Côte des Blancs. Edgar Ruinart died young, in 1881, at the age of fifty-three. It does not seem that he enjoyed good health; and in his portrait he looks rather pale, gloomy and severe, despite the studied elegance of his dark

Recreation of old champagne-making skills in the cellars of the Maison Ruinart: on the left, the process of *remuage* on a wooden rack; and on the right, corking.

clothes. He had kept the Maison Ruinart in good shape, without showing much commercial flair: in spite of the visit to Russia, which did not bring him the benefits that he was no doubt hoping for. His only great success had been the spectacular breakthrough in the English market, which was to retain its predominant position until the end of the century. He left no children. His marriage with Mina Sheppard had not been a success. The couple separated in 1867, and from then on led independent lives, with Edgar in Reims, and his wife mainly in Paris, in the Avenue Montaigne. But during a voyage to England in 1870, Edgar visited a convent and decided to bring back to France a fatherless girl, whose mother, finding herself in financial difficulties, agreed to part with her daughter on condition that the Vicomte Ruinart would see to her education. It would not be impossible to speculate idly on the origin of this child, and to ask whether she was Edgar's natural daughter: the claim has already been made, in spite of the lack of proof. And there is no lack of circumstantial evidence. The young Mary Kate Riboldi, normally called Charlotte, was brought up by Edgar Ruinart as his own daughter, went to the best schools, and was entrusted to the best tutors; and she was treated as his daughter by the family and by Reims society. So it is not surprising that when he died, Edgar left most of his considerable fortune to this more-or-less adopted daughter. Although he named his older brother Charles as sole legatee, the extent of the individual bequests (including 1,500,000 francs to Charlotte) effectively left Charles with just the Maison Ruinart business. At this point Edgar's widow appeared, contesting the will under the pretext of championing the interests of the young girl, whom she claimed to have been wronged by Charles and the executors of the will—all people of the utmost probity. Assuming that Charlotte was Edgar's natural daughter, this was a comic situation. There followed a legal battle that has no relevance to the story of the Maison Ruinart Père & Fils, but which is reminiscent of Eugène Sue and *Les Mystères de Paris*, with English lawyers, guardian-claimants (also English, and none too disinterested), the real mother appearing to order from the slums of London, the procuction of letters from the Mother Superior of the Filles de la Charité, etc.

In the end, the matter was settled as in the best novels: André Ruinart de Brimont, Charles' son and heir, duly fell for the young and ravishing orphan, and married her—which, incidentally, had the effect of putting the family fortune back together under the same roof.

So in 1881 Charles found himself heir to the business that he had left under his brother's control twenty-five years before, and he now set to work—if that is the right expression—in the offices of the Rue Crayère. Although the archives do not provide detailed information on the short period—seven years—when Charles was nominally head of the Maison Ruinart, it does seem that he preferred life in Paris to life in Reims. But his son André—the fourth of seven children from his marriage (1854) to Alice Hennessy, from the famous cognac family—became a partner at a young age, and seems to have been more motivated and also more knowledgeable about the champagne trade. He also moved into the family's *hôtel particulier* in the Rue Monsieur—a house full of age-old business associations. Economically, these were difficult times, in France as abroad. Charles' approach was not entirely in tune with the times. He spurned small orders, and saw fit to deliver only the larger ones. So to a person wanting to buy a dozen bottles, he replied, "We do not accept orders for 12 bottles, and suggest you contact your grocer."

The Vicomtesse Charles Ruinart de Brimont, née Hennessy, wife of Charles, holding her daughter Sophie (later Mme Auguste Ouizille) on her knees.
Archives Ruinart, Reims.

The Bubbles of the Second Empire

The sentiment was concisely put, but no longer acceptable at the end of the nineteenth century.

It was no doubt for these reasons that on 20 October 1888, Charles Ruinart de Brimont virtually handed over the Maison Ruinart to his son Ancré, creating with him a new company in the place of the old one, together also with two partners from Reims: Thierry Frédéric Lelarge, manufacturer, and Alphonse Firmin Charbonneaux, master glassmaker. Largely thanks to his wife's fortune, André bought this last partner's share in the partnership. He brought 2,100,000 francs to the company, and was easily the controlling partner; and his father brought the establishment in the Rue des Crayères, the cellars, and the plant and equipment necessary to carry on the business. Charles now left to live in Paris, where he had a flat in the Rue Cimarosa, and no longer involved himself in the running of the Maison Ruinart, from which he received a private income until he died in 1896.

The Maison Ruinart Père & Fils now entered a new phase. It was run by a man who had the fibre of his ancestors, and who faced the task of reinvigorating the business in spite of the hazards of the economic situation and the problems that his father and uncle—who lacked the drive of their predecessors—had had to deal with. He was to show himself equal to the task, which unfortunately time and the First World War were not to allow him to finish off.

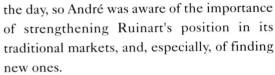

Supplier to Courts...

At the age of twenty-seven
—he was born in 1861—
André Ruinartde Brimont took the reins of the
Maison Ruinart, determined to put new life into a business that, to his
mind, was relying too much on the efforts made by his great-grandfather Irénée. In this end of the century period, the competition between
champagne producers was harsher, and protectionism was the order of

the day, so André was aware of the importance
of strengthening Ruinart's position in its
traditional markets, and, especially, of finding
new ones.

Exports were hardly encouraged by the
denouncement, in 1881, of the old commercial
treaties between France and her trading partners, and by the considerable increase in customs duties, which more or less doubled in
1882, from 8-15% to 15-30%. This measure
was a particularly unwelcome development for
Ruinart Père & Fils, who for almost one and a
half centuries had relied heavily on foreign
trade.

The political background did not alleviate
these economic constraints. England was a
striking example. In 1882, developments in
Egypt and the Suez led to increasing antago-
nism, even hostility, between the two powers.
The effect on commerce was clearly visible:
Ruinart's exports to Great Britain in general
and London in particular, now fell to a quarter of what they had been in
the previous decade. So the proportion of the Maison Ruinart's total
sales going to England now began to fall, too—and at three quarters, it
had undeniably been too high. In the first years of the twentieth century, this proportion settled at around two fifths, which was still high.
So England remained the favoured market of the Maison Ruinart. And
Ruinart was so popular there that it even featured in a song:

*I invited him to dinner
in a place I knew near Kempton Park,
and I told him that the wine was Ruinart
—I had changed the name on the bottle—.
"You are lying," said this Sherlock Holmes.
"This wine costs 36 pennies
I know from the cork
that I found on the floor."*

With the help of his colleagues—including his assistant J. Max Leroy and his head cellarman Maurice Hazart, whose family had worked for the Maison Ruinart for several generations—André Ruinart now set out to strengthen the business' position everywhere abroad. Circumstances were very much changed, and the Maison Ruinart could not hope to trade on past glory.

Three countries illustrate the new situation.

First of all there was the German Empire, made up of a number of kingdoms and grand duchies that enjoyed a certain amount of independence whilst recognising—often unwillingly—the sovereignty of the King of Prussia. The order books feature the Crown Prince Wilhelm—future Wilhelm II—and also his cousins Prince Frederick and, more importantly for Ruinart, Prince Carl von Hohenzollern in Potsdam, from whom the flow of orders stopped only in 1913. The list of clients also included the Chancellor of the Empire, Prince von Hohenlohe-Schillingsfurst, who was faithful to Ruinart throughout his career: as Prime Minister of Bavaria, then German Ambassador in Paris, after that Governor of Alsace-Lorraine, and finally Chancellor until 1900; and there were the Count von Lerchenfeld-Koefering, and the Count von Brühl. But for the Maison Ruinart, the main factor in Germany was Bavaria, and its Court and royal family. Indeed, the Wittelsbach family were the Maison Ruinart's best clients: King Otto (1848-1913), the Prince-Regent Luitpold (1821-1912), the Duke Karl-Theodor, and the Duke Ludwig-Wilhelm.

Naturally, the royal family brought a clientèle in their wake, which included aristocrats, but was made up mainly of the *bourgeoisie* and established institutions such as the Gesellschafts Museum and the Akademischer Philisterwerbank, both in Munich; and away from the capital,

List of wines sold by the Maison Ruinart Père & Fils in 1899. *Archives Ruinart, Reims.*

97

**Letter dated
4 March 1898 from
the Grand Master of
the Court of Bavaria,
informing
André Ruinart of his
appointment as
"Supplier to the
Court".**
*Archives Ruinart,
Reims.*

there were restaurants and hotels, especially in the country's numerous health resorts.

Now that it had been present in Bavaria for almost a century, the Maison Ruinart was rewarded by the title and position of "Suppliers to the Court", which was granted to the head of the Maison Ruinart Père & Fils, by Prince Luitpold, Regent of the Kingdom acting for the unfortunate King Otto, who was shut away in a madhouse, like his brother King Louis II before him. The official warrant announcing the appointment was sent to André Ruinart de Brimont by the Grand Master of the Court on 7 March 1898, and the news was published on the 13th in the *Münchner Neueste Nachrichten*. This honour reflected a recognised position, and should have helped Ruinart's business not only in the Kingdom, but also beyond its borders. Strangely, it does not seem that this was the case.

There were, however, places where Ruinart flowed in rivers: military casinos, in other words German officers' messes, which, especially since the occupation of France during the Franco-Prussian War, seemed not to be able to do without Ruinart's champagne—which in 1896 was stocked by fifteen *casinos*, notably in Munich, Frankfurt, Amberg, Augsburg, and also Metz, now part of the German Empire. Nor was this fashion limited to Germany, since Ruinart champagne was ordered in England and throughout the Commonwealth by the officers of the Queen's army; and by the officers of the armies of the Tsar of Russia and the King of the Belgians.

And in the Belgian market, Ruinart had been a supplier to the Court since 1874. But Leopold II, King of the Belgians, was hardly ordering anything—he did not have his father's fondness for Ruinart. On the other hand, Prince Eugène de Ligne in Brussels continued the tradition of his family and his grandfather, the famous Prince Joseph.

The officers of the Ligne Regiment also drank Ruinart, just like their fellow-officers in the Royal Guard at Laeken and in the Grenadiers. Other Belgian clients included the Baron de Macar in Brussels, the Comte de Pinto in Ensival, the Comte Vilain at the Château de Basel-lez-Tamise, and the Comte Cornet in Laeken.

Then there was the Russian market, which now, at the end of the century, was picking up; or rather, growing. If the Tsar Alexander II had not viewed France with the most approving of eyes, the same was not true of his son and successor Alexander III, who came to the throne in 1881. This bearded giant, fiercely autocratic and Slavophile, admired France for the civilising influence of her culture—not for her form of government, since the very word "republic" filled him with horror. It was he, however, who forged the Franco-Russian Alliance of 1891.

André Ruinart was not slow to increase his efforts to seek out business in the Empire of the Tsars.

His clients were mainly restaurant-owners, and, as in Germany and Belgium, officers. The books show deliveries to various officers' messes: the Sappers of the St. Petersburg Guard in 1897-1898; and in 1904, to the Horse Guards and the Mounted Guards, elite cavalry regiments of the Imperial Guard. Deliveries made in these high military circles were an introduction to the Russian aristocracy: and amongst Ruinart's private clients was Prince Viazemsky—who was very bad at settling accounts.

A bottle of Ruinart champagne, ten yards high, displayed at the Universal Exhibition in Brussels in 1897.
Archives Ruinart, Reims.

Business in Russia went well: in 1897 alone, Ruinart's turnover in St. Petersburg was 17,300 francs, and sales in Moscow were equal to those in Warsaw.

Due to the active and long-term presence of competitors, the Russian market, perhaps more than others, needed to be looked after by an determined local agent. And following the arrival in St. Petersburg, at the beginning of this century, of a new agent, Pierre du Bellet, the Maison Ruinart was able to increase its presence in the Russian market during the reign of Nicholas II. Refined, cultivated, and well-connected, he did invaluable work for Ruinart which the First World War and the Revolution completely destroyed. The beautiful, almost literary presentation of his business reports sets him apart from all Ruinart's other foreign agents (see the Appendix: Ruinart in Russia).

Apart from these three large countries that illustrate nature of Ruinart's activities, the Maison Ruinart was present in numerous places elsewhere, although not always with the same degree of success. Exports to the United States were almost non-existent, the only significant sales in the continent of North America being to Canada. Africa opened up a bit: in 1896 there were several orders from Matadi in the Congo, mainly from French engineers abroad, for whom a bottle of Ruinart no doubt brought back memories of the *douceur de vivre* of their homeland. The customs war of 1888 between France and Italy meant that there

99

A hoarding
advertising Ruinart's
champagne.
Kameniostrovsky
Prospect, June 1901.
*Archives Ruinart,
Reims.*

were no longer any clients there. As for Switzerland, Geneva made a tentative appearance, with orders from the Prince von Oldenburg in 1897-1898. There is little information about Spain, but there were sales there, since on 23 December 1904 André Ruinart once more obtained the grant of the title "Supplier to the Royal Household", communicated to him in the name of King Alphonse XIII by the Marquess of Bonje, Master of the Royal Household. The warrant stated that:
"His Majesty the King, Our Master (may God protect him) has pleasure in granting your request, and hereby permits you to use the Royal coat of arms on invoices and labels of the champagne-producing house that you own in your town. May God protect you."

❧ André Ruinart de Brimont
was not only a shrewd manager and businessman: he also understood communications, in advance of his time. And he appreciated the importance of sponsorship, which he decided to exercise in an

area in which the public was then passionately interested: the novel world of aviation.

Since the Wright brothers' first flight in 1903, these "madmen flying their strange contraptions" had experienced the thrill of an exciting and heroic period. Everyone was talking about legendary or soon-to-be legendary figures: Santos-Dumont, Blériot, Farman, Latham, Garros, Delagrange, Véndrines, Chavez—and many others besides.

In 1906, André Ruinart decided to take part in this extraordinary adventure. He believed in the future. Since he had no desire to become an aviator himself, he did not get involved personally; but he set out to offer his assistance to avaitors. He therefore created the Ruinart Père & Fils Cup whose rules were registered with the International Aeronautical Federation. The definitive terms of this prize were fixed on 4 December 1906.

The competition was open to all aviators, "without distinction of nationality", until 1 January 1910, offering a prize for crossing the Channel "in a machine heavier than air, and propelled independently of outside agencies", the starting point being either in England or in France.

Notification of the day of the attempted crossing had to be given in writing sixty days before the event, with a further signed confirmation to be given forty-eight hours before. Then came an astonishing condition: attempts could only be made at the weekend.

Attempts were to be supervised by the Aero-Club of France. And the prize consisted of an impressive silver cup and 12,500 francs, or £500 sterling. It was a tidy sum for the period, and would doubtless be most useful for the winner.

Collerette, designed for the *Carte Anglaise* vintage, 1901. *Archives Ruinart, Reims.*

To most people, and to aviators in particular, these conditions seemed severe, even draconian. And some thought that they were hopelessly unrealistic. The motors of the time—on which any crossing would rely—were capricious, and it appeared impossible to fix the date of an attempted flight two months in advance. One journalist went so far as to suggest that André Ruinart surely believed in flying carpets and the tales of the *Thousand and One Nights*.

Nevertheless, aviation was progressing. And in 1908 the *Daily Mail* created a similar prize, with more lenient conditions, for the same feat: flying across the Channel. So when on 25 July 1909, Blériot successfully made a flight between Calais and Dover, he qualified for the *Daily Mail*'s prize, but not for Ruinart's one. André Ruinart must have regretted this, since otherwise his own name and that of the Maison Ruinart would have been linked to Blériot's historic crossing of the Channel. In any case, he now realised that this crossing was not just a mere matter of twenty-two miles, and he reduced the notice to be given from sixty days to ten.

Then a certain Jacques de Lesseps set out to win the prize, and fixed the date of his attempt for Saturday 14 May 1910. He was young — twenty-seven years old—tall, thin, and wore a moustache, like André Ruinart. His was a son of the famous Ferdinand, the engineer who had made the Suez Canal.

He was Blériot's first pupil, and had been a pilot for only a few months—his pilot's licence bore the number 27. He had got it in January of that year, and since then had been doing practice runs from the aerodrome at Issy-les-Moulineaux, on the outskirts of Paris. He had already taken part in several events. Lesseps was preparing to leave for Calais when the death of King Edward VII was announced, and since there was no question of undertaking the flight when England was in mourning, André Ruinart agreed to put forward the date of the attempt a few days, to 21 May. So on the 20th, the pilot left for Calais with his team of mechanics. He was also accompanied by journalists, supporters, his brother Bertrand de Lesseps, his brother-in-law M. de Miramon, and André Ruinart and his wife and closest colleagues. The group reached a spot known as Les Baraques, near the Grignon dairy. This was the place from which Blériot had taken off less than a year ago. The aeroplane, a Blériot XI with a 50 horse-power Gnome and Rhône *Scarabée* engine, was put together, and the mechanics passed a good part of the night checking and testing, with the Ruinart limousines parked outside the nearby farm.

On the morning of Saturday 21 May, Les Baraques was invaded by crowds; but there was a 35 mph wind, and they had to wait. In the middle of the afternoon, the wind finally fell, only to be replaced by fog. All the same, Jacques de Lesseps was ready. Chatting and laughing with André Ruinart, he put on a blue flying suit and donned his helmet. In their blue and white uniforms, the sailors of the escort ship La Lance held back the crowd, and protected the monoplane and its pilot, who cleared a path through the spectators for take-off. At 3.48 pm the motor started up, and the Blériot leapt forward and made a

21 May 1905, in the place known as Les Baraques, near Calais. Jacques de Lesseps, wearing a flying suit, prepares for his historic crossing of the Channel in a Blériot XI. Beside him, camera in hand, is André Ruinart de Brimont, who was to be one of the sponsors of the famous Aviation Week, an important event in the emerging world of aviation.
Archives Ruinart, Reims.

smooth take-off to the accompaniment of cheers from the crowd: he was on his way to England. In spite of the stormy sky, Jacques de Lesseps reached a height of 750 metres between the fog and the blue sky. Down below, in the Channel, the destroyer *Escopette* and the tug *Calasien* were ready to pick up the pilot if necessary. Forty-two minutes later, after a flight at an average speed of almost forty miles an hour, the triumphant Blériot landed in a field near St. Margaret's Bay, to the north-east of Dover. This Frenchman fallen from the sky was welcomed by the inhabitants of a nearby cottage who were enjoying a cup of tea.

Although Jacques de Lesseps did not conceal his joy at having won the Ruinart Cup, he almost immediately started prepartions for the return flight, sparing hardly a moment to talk to his admirers. But the fog became more and more thick, so he had to give up thoughts of leaving that evening. He was still there on Sunday. So Lesseps decided to return to France by boat, and he boarded the Escopette, where André and Mme Ruinart were waiting for him, and together they headed back to Calais. And there, disappointed for the second time by the unpre-

Collectors' stamps
designed by Debar
and commissioned
by André Ruinart,
to commemorate
the crossing of the
Channel by Jacques
de Lesseps on
21 May 1910 (above)
and by Charles Rolls
on 2 June 1910
(below).
*Archives Ruinart,
Reims.*

dictability of the winds, a crowd of ten thousand people was waiting for him at the quayside. There, too, surrounded by the representatives of the Aero-Club of France, André Ruinart de Brimont formally presented him with the cup and a cheque.

One week later, on 28 May, an English pilot attempted to win the Ruinart Cup. Six years older than Jacques de Lesseps, the Hon. Charles Rolls, son of Lord Llangattock, had been to Eton and Cambridge. He was an electrical engineer. But his overriding passion was for cars. He had already taken part in numerous international events, and since 1903 had been the holder of the world speed record (83 mph). In 1904, he and Frederick Henry Royce founded what was to become the most prestigious make of car in the world: Rolls Royce. But Rolls was interested in aeroplanes, too: he was one of the founders of the Aero-Club of England, and made numerous ascents in balloons. He was the first Englishman to fly, owned a Wright aeroplane, introduced almost the entire English aristocracy to aviation, and in 1909 even obtained a French pilot's licence (number 23). He became a member of the Aero-Club of France.

After an unsuccessful attempt on 21 May, Rolls tried again on 2 June 1910. He left from Dover at 6.30 pm in a sky so clear that the English onlookers could follow his aeroplane until it was within five miles of the French coast. Having arrived above land, near Calais, at 7.05, he flew over Sangatte and transmitted a message to the Aero-Club of France before heading back to England. He reached the cliffs of Dover at 8.02, and landed four minutes later. He was the first person to have completed a non-stop return journey between France and England. André Ruinart gave him a cup, admittedly rather more modest than the one he had awarded to Jacques de Lesseps. But Rolls did not survive his achievement for long, and was killed one month later at an event in Bournemouth.

André Ruinart had therefore linked the name of the Maison Ruinart to the new world of aviation. He did not stop at that, and was also one of the sponsors of the annual Aviation Week that took place at Reims.

To commemorate this double success, he commissioned a Reims artist to design two stamp-shaped vignettes with illustrations of aeroplanes above the Channel. And again with an eye to publicity, it was André Ruinart who commissioned the famous artist Alphonse Mucha to design the Ruinart poster with a young auburn-haired woman draped in yellow, champagne glass in hand—a poster that was to be displayed in countless fashionable cafés and restaurants. And strangely enough, the *Mucha*, as this poster came to be called, was even to be found at the top of Mont Blanc, stuck to the wooden wall of a mountain hut by a champagne-loving climber.

The Maison Ruinart's commercial literature also reflected this desire to communicate—which was in any case necessary, since the strict legislation of the time obliged champagne producers to spell out the distinction between their product and the so-called vins mousseux. The famous Délimitation de la Champagne law dates from 12 February 1912. But from 1911 onwards, Ruinart's clients were liable to read sentences such as "We would inform our clients that we are applying the law in advance, and that from now on the word Champagne will feature on all the labels of the bottles that leave our Reims cellars. This will offer an absolute guarantee of authenticity."

And the following invitation was appended: "We would like to remind our clients that our Cellars, generally recognised as being the most picturesque in Champagne, are open to visitors passing through Reims, and that we will always be most glad to show you around."

A few months later, during the end-of-year festivities, the tone was even more direct: "We enclose our current price-list. All our wines are, of course, authentic *vins de Champagne*, which should not be confused with the cheap and indiscriminately marketed *vins mousseux* of undetermined origin."

In May 1912, the Maison Ruinart, decidedly unhappy about the unfair competition from these *mousseux*, returned to the attack: "If the label does not carry the word Champagne, then the wine is not authentic wine from Champagne, even if the bottle suggests that it is—this sort of wine can only be sold as *vin mousseux*."

"As for our own products, we would merely remind our clients that, as in the past, we sell only authentic *vins de Champagne*. The extent of our stocks and reserves—almost unrivalled in Champagne—puts us in an excellent position (in spite of the present crisis) to ensure that our wines continue to be undisputedly of the highest possible quality."

"PS: All our corks bear the date of the foundation of the Maison Ruinart: 1729."

The famous Ruinart poster designed by Alphonse Mucha, and subsequently known in the champagne world simply as the *Mucha*. *Archives Ruinart, Reims.*

Ruinart's Belle Epoque
designs for menus.
*Archives Ruinart,
Reims.*

Ruinart Père & Fils now offered a range of five *cuvées* to their clients: pride of place still went to the famous La Maréchale, a *grand vin* "in the French taste"—as the advertisements put it—whose name derived from the distinguished vineyard at Sillery that had once belonged to the Maréchale d'Estrées. But André Ruinart had sold part of this symbolic vineyard on taking over the running of the Maison Ruinart. This was a significant action, showing a desire to move with the times by disposing of a vineyard whose upkeep was too expensive. From now on, Ruinart increasingly tended to buy almost all their wines from independent producers. The wholesalers paid eight and a half francs for a bottle of La Maréchale. One of the menus designed for Ruinart and offered to restaurant-owners carried an illustration of the Marshal's wife walking around her vineyard in a dress with panniers. André Ruinart was clearly a firm believer in the emerging art of advertising.

Next came the *Extra Quality Dry*, a very high quality dry wine; and then a *vin brut* "in the American taste"—so called because of its great popularity in the United States. These two wines both cost eight and a half francs, also. The *Carte Anglaise*, a great favourite with the English, and again very dry, was at nine francs the most expensive wine sold by the Maison Ruinart, and always carried the year. And at the other end of the scale, the *Carte Blanche* was described as a *demi-sec* wine "of excellent quality, and very reasonably priced".

❦ 1913: the last year of the old order, which was to vanish for good in August 1914. Afterwards, nothing would ever be the same again—neither lifestyles, nor fortunes, nor clients.

The world of Ruinart Père & Fils had changed noticeably since the beginning of the century.

But their most important foreign market was still Great Britain, where sales benefited from the policy of entente and friendly exchange pursued by the British government, and marked by the settlement of colonial disputes in 1904, and the conference at Algesiras in 1906. From now on, most of the market was centred on London, which overshadowed cities like Liverpool, Carlisle, Newcastle and Edinburgh.

Munich continued to dominate the German market, followed by Rastatt in the Grand Duchy of Baden, and Vienna, leader of the Austrian market, which was showing a renewed interest in Ruinart. But sales in Prussia had now almost come to a halt.

The kingdoms of northern Europe were still only small clients. But there were some sales in Oslo and Trondheim in Norway, which Ruinart had visited for the first time. And thanks to the commercial determination of M. du Bellay, Russia was an increasingly important market. The market in southern Europe consisted mainly of Spain—the two key cities of Barcelona and Madrid, the capital—and Italy, now opening up again to Ruinart, especially in the north, where Milan was the hub. Sales were made even in out-of-the-way villages, which bears witness to an attempt to create a wider market.

Exports were increasingly steadily to Belgium, where Liège was now a far more important client than Brussels. The main development in foreign markets was the increasing importance of outlets in the United States, represented mainly by New York, Philadelphia and Chicago, from where wholesalers sold Ruinart's products on to other clients. The success in America was mainly due to the Roosevelt & Schyler partnership, Ruinart's exclusive agents in the United States (Roosevelt was the uncle of the future President of the United States).

This Exquisite Wine of Champagne. Score of the drinking song written by J. L. Mac Evoy in 1894, and published in the United States. Archives Ruinart, Reims.

And finally, some sales bore witness to the expansionist policies of the Maison Ruinart: Piraeus, Johannesburg in South Africa, and even Hong Kong. Thanks to the dynamism of André Ruinart, the French market was developing. Sales drives were carried out in a systematic way, both in areas where the Maison Ruinart traditionally had a hold, like the north, and in new ones too. And so the accounts for this period regularly show sales to the Côte d'Azur (Nice, Cannes, Monte-Carlo), the coast towns on the Channel (Saint-Malo, Cayeux-sur-Mer, Mers-les-Bains, Boulogne-sur-Mer, Berck-Plage), and also those in the Pays Basque (Biarritz, Perpignan): these seaside resorts, whose fashionability was now established for good, attracted a well-off and free-spending clientèle. Paris remained in the lead, followed by Lyons, which had regained the position lost at the beginning of the nineteenth century.

The private clientèle was much less aristocratic, and came mainly from the commercial *bourgeoisie*; and the hotels and restaurants that bought from Ruinart tended increasingly to belong to the luxury category.

Grape-pickers' baskets outside a barn at Sillery before the First World War. Archives Ruinart, Reims.

❧ The First World War killed the momentum established by André Ruinart de Brimont and his business. At the beginning of the summer, clients were informed that due to the fall in the level of stocks, the price of vintage wines would rise slightly. This was the sign of a firm market. Europe was dancing on the edge of a volcano, drinking the last glasses of champagne before the catastrophe. In August, sales came to a complete halt. They only started up again, in a trickle, in April 1915: but with small deliveries to Sweden, which remained a neutral country, Johannesburg, and Brussels.

Being fifty-three years old, André Ruinart was not called up to fight —but he fought, in his own way, at the head of his business. Reims was under bombardment, and the town was at the heart of the fighting. The aeroplanes of the two opposing sides flew daily over the roofs and belltowers of the cathedral. Day by day, Reims became a martyred town; roads and entire neighbourhoods disappeared, destroyed by shells or fire.

The buildings on the Saint-Nicaise mound and in the Rue des Crayères, dating back to the eighteenth century and occupied since then by Ruinart Père & Fils, were hit several times. The roofs collapsed; shells pockmarked the walls, destroyed the storerooms, knocked down the courtyard buildings and made craters in the ground. Only the cellars in the famous chalk mines stood firm against the blasts and explosions. As in Roman times, they became a place of shelter and refuge. The population of Reims congregated there, safe under the white vaults that shook at the blasts, but did not collapse. Naturally, André Ruinart moved his offices there—files and furniture were all carried down. And there, in the dim glow of electric lights or paraffin lamps, he continued to direct his business with his colleagues beside him. When a shell burst a main and the water began flooding in, he put his table on a makeshift raft and philosophically carried on with his work while the water was pumped out. When he went up above ground, it was to see new damage—the old buildings were reduced to ruins. Being an active man, he no doubt wondered when circumstances would

The head office of Ruinart Père & Fils, in the Rue des Crayères, after the bombings of 1918. Archives Ruinart, Reims.

NEXT PAGE
Ruinart's cellars in the Gallo-Roman chalk mines. *Archives Ruinart, Reims.*

allow him to start rebuilding. But four years living underground in constant humidity got the better of his health. Although he survived the interminable war, he did not live for long after: his lungs had been destroyed, and he died on 11 October 1919.

So died one of the great heads of the Maison Ruinart—a cultivated and modern man, accessible to new ideas. During his thirty-one years in charge of the business, from 1888 to 1919, he had put it back on its feet, and, to borrow M. Decrock's words, had put a stop to the commercial paralysis that had seemed to overcome his nineteenth-century predecessors Edmond, Edgar, and Charles Ruinart, whose hopes and—to some extent—hearts had never left the eighteenth century.

Collerette, bearing the Ruinart coat of arms. *Archives Ruinart, Reims.*

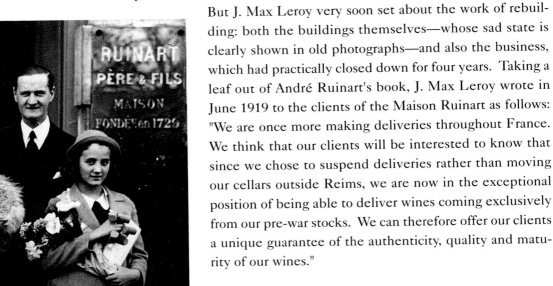

❦ The early death
of André Ruinart de Brimont was to have dire

consequences for the Maison Ruinart. Only someone of his strong personality could have coped with the post-war difficulties. In spite of the presence of J. Max Leroy, the gap that he left could not be filled.

But J. Max Leroy very soon set about the work of rebuilding: both the buildings themselves—whose sad state is clearly shown in old photographs—and also the business, which had practically closed down for four years. Taking a leaf out of André Ruinart's book, J. Max Leroy wrote in June 1919 to the clients of the Maison Ruinart as follows: "We are once more making deliveries throughout France. We think that our clients will be interested to know that since we chose to suspend deliveries rather than moving our cellars outside Reims, we are now in the exceptional position of being able to deliver wines coming exclusively from our pre-war stocks. We can therefore offer our clients a unique guarantee of the authenticity, quality and maturity of our wines."

Gérard Ruinart de Brimont (1902-1975), photographed in 1937. He was the last head of the Maison Ruinart to bear the family name. *Archives Ruinart, Reims.*

Prices went up, too: *La Maréchale*, the *Extra Quality Dry* and the American *vin brut* rose from 8.50 francs to 15 francs; the 1906 *Carte Anglaise* rose from 10.50 francs to 18 francs; the *Carte Blanche* went up from 6 francs to 12 francs; and the new 1911 *Carte Anglaise* was put on the market at 17 francs. Overall, the average price rise was over 80%.

But although it was large enough, this price rise doubtless failed to cover expenses, particularly labour costs: from 1 September 1919 there was a further across-the-board price rise of about one franc.

The Maison Ruinart Père & Fils also had to set about rebuilding their network of agents. In this post-war period where only the soldiers had gained credit, newcomers were judged partly on their military record. So when informing his clients of the appointment of the new general agent for Belgium, J. Max Leroy did not fail to spell out the agent's credentials in this respect:

"It has been a source of great pleasure to us to note that our appointment of M. Bosquet—a volunteer in the Belgian army during the war, and holder of the War Cross and the Yser Medal—has met with the entire approval of our faithful and long-standing clientèle."

It was then that the widow of André Ruinart de Brimont showed her mettle. In December 1920, the clients of the Maison Ruinart, and the champagne world and the business world in general, learnt that the Vicomtesse André had set up a new company called "Champagne Ruinart Ruinart Père & Fils, successors", with a capital of four million francs (1920). She was to be chairman on behalf of her son Gérard, the last Ruinart of their branch of the family, then aged eighteen (he was born in 1902). The board appointed J. Max Leroy as director of the company, and F. Sérinet as the board's representative. Like a true regent of this family kingdom, the Vicomtesse André set out her intentions briefly: "I have created this new company mainly to help my son take charge of his father's affairs when he reaches the age to do so. The new company incorporates the old Maison Ruinart Ruinart Père & Fils, and will respect its traditions scrupulously." The signature below belongs to a strong-charactered woman, a far cry from the poor English orphan who had been adopted by Charles Ruinart: the former boarder at the Roule convent in Paris had become head of the family.

Label for Ruinart's *vin brut* sold in the United States. 1906. *Archives Ruinart, Reims.*

J. Max Leroy, who oversaw the interim period between the death of André Ruinart de Brimont and the coming of age of his son Gérard. *Archives Ruinart, Reims.*

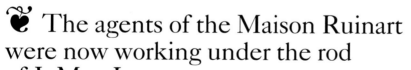

❦ The agents of the Maison Ruinart were now working under the rod of J. Max Leroy. Business was extremely tough. Prices

had been put up again in November 1920, and at their new level they discouraged sales. Therefore in December 1921 they were reduced, so that a bottle of *La Maréchale*, which had been priced at 22.50 francs, now came down to 17.50 francs, with all other cuvées being reduced in proportion. In order to encourage sales, the agents were already talking about the "almost two hundred-year-old" reputation of the Maison Ruinart—a full eight years before the bicentary!

Pencil in the shape
of a Ruinart bottle,
1923.
*Archives Ruinart,
Reims.*

A series of postcards of the chalk mines was issued: they showed the rows of bottles on racks in these immense cellars where every gallery bore the name of one of the heads of the Maison Ruinart. There were galleries named after Claude, Irénée, Nicolas, Edmond, and lastly, André—this one reached a height of thirty-eight metres.

The inventiveness of the management of the Maison Ruinart manifested itself in what is nowadays known as promotion: so in 1923, they had a supply of pencils made in the shape of a Ruinart champagne bottle, to give to clients.

Guided tours of the chalk mines were now a normal part of business life. Groups of tourists or people in the wine trade came to spend a few hours under the immense vaults, and to drink a glass of champagne; and they generally left with a few bottles. The photo-souvenir had become a rite: from 1925, after Gérard Ruinart had formally taken control of the Maison Ruinart (which was still effectively run by J. Max Leroy), he often posed behind these groups, towering above the visitors, whose faces were smiling after a visit ending with a champagne tasting session, or even a fine meal served in a gallery specially adapted for the occasion. Everything was perfectly organised: a few days after their visit, the companies or groups received framed and dated photographs, or even a souvenir album.

A Ruinart stand
in Brussels
in the 1920's.
*Archives Ruinart,
Reims.*

Alhough the cellars and the stores of course stayed at the Rue des Crayères, the offices had been moved to André Ruinart de Brimont's *hôtel particulier* in the Boulevard Lundy, ten minutes away from Saint-Nicaise. It was here that Gérard lived, in a vast and magnificent forty-five-room building with the family coat of arms on the façade, and designed for his parents in 1896 by the architect Paul Blondel, winner of the Grand Prix de Rome.

All the same, sales hardly picked up. Prices had to be raised: in January 1926, the vintage *brut* sold at 26 francs, and *La Maréchale* at 21 francs; and in July, *La Maréchale* rose to 26 francs, and the 1921 vintage to 34.50 francs. Even these prices were subject to sudden changes, due to the marked instability of the exchange rate.

The harvest of 1926 turned out to be very bad, and stocks fell. The price of the 1921 *brut* continued to rise, and reached 42 francs in Octo-

Façade of the Hôtel du Lundy, built in 1896 for the Vicomte André Ruinart de Brimont, on the Boulevard Lundy in Reims. This detail shows the family coat of arms sculpted in stone above the balcony of the first floor. The Hôtel du Lundy now belongs to the town of Reims.

The offices of Roosevelt & Schwyler, Ruinart's Chicago agents, at 223 Michigan Avenue, in the 1920's. *Archives Ruinart, Reims.*

ber: it had risen by 7.50 francs in three months. Ruinart had truly set out on a journey across the desert, and the fact that most other champagne producers were in the same position did not make things any easier.

British advertisement for Ruinart's *Carte Anglaise*. Singapore, 1930's. *Archives Ruinart, Reims.*

❧ The international situation now offered a far from encouraging background for the exports on which Ruinart had traditionally built its name. In England, the most important foreign market, the agents came and went: Hall & Grey (until 1923), Robertson Bros. & Co. (1923-1936), Atkinson, Baldwin & Co. (1936-1938), and then Anderson, Dobson & Co. from 1938. Then there was the general agent for Ireland, a certain English (strangely enough), based in Dublin. This succession of agents suggests that business was far from easy across the Channel from France.

In the United States, the momentum of the pre-war years, that had almost turned the country into Ruinart's biggest export market, ended in prohibition: the consumption of alcohol was banned everywhere. This resulted in a complete halt to Ruinart's exports there. The Depression of 1929 only made matters worse.

There was also a change of agents in Belgium, with Octave Bosquet representing the Maison Ruinart there from 1919 to 1920, followed by Léon de Savignac from then on: he was active in seeking out business, and showed initiative. Ruinart's presence was maintained in the northern markets by Oskar Kolby in Norway, and also by Sloos in Holland—the latter being replaced in 1926 by Anthony Nolet in Nimègue. In Switzerland the Maison Ruinart was represented by Lambert Picard in Lausanne, and by Marc Poggi, then by Arthur Sassoon, and finally by Edmond Charlus in Geneva. In Marocco the agent was Maurice Bouvier-Bangillon, and in Algiers, René Berger. And sales in Austria were the responsibility of Albert Schlesinger in Vienna, and of Hans Menshausen in Berlin.

The Russian market of course collapsed with the 1917 Revolution: the USSR was not as keen on champagne as the Russia of the Tsars, and

from now on sweet sparkling wines known as "Crimea champagne" started to invade the palaces of the new rulers, and have still not yet been dislodged.

So the foreign markets contracted inexorably between the wars, and Ruinart was once more obliged to look to the French market, which if not marginal until then, had at any rate been considerably less lively.

The network of general agents was relatively dense, and covered a good part of the country: Rouiller, Brion, Amette, and Cealis in Paris; Ducrot in Annecy; the Seignouret brothers in Bordeaux; Joannon in Marseille; Dreumont in Cambrai; Colas and then Pariset in Lyonss; Roux in Grenoble; Baschamp in Nantes; Clapisson in Valenciennes; Badie in Perpignan; Papineau in Besançon; Nicolas in Lille; Ploix in Fougères; Pichon in Rouen; Wattel-Ernould in Roubaix; Dugelay in Montauban; Delahaye in Lille; Charbonnier in Charleville; Flagollet in Le Havre; and Chameroy in La Baule. There were hardly any regions that were not covered by Ruinart.

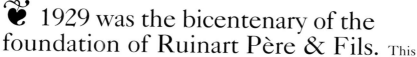

1929 was the bicentenary of the foundation of Ruinart Père & Fils. This

event is referred to in commercial literature, on the menus designed for Ruinart for use in restaurants, and on the postcards of the chalk mines. But no special event marked the anniversary. It was not until 1937 that a *Special Bicentenary Cuvée, Vin Brut 1929* was put on the market, and in very limited quantities, to enhance its value: 62,500 bottles, and 19,500 half-bottles, all numbered. In keeping with standards that Ruinart respects to this day, this *cuvée* was made of only the very best growths from Champagne. It was put on the market at 35 francs a bottle, and the next year went up to 38.50 francs, then to 42 francs. It was also in 1937 that a vignette showing a portrait of the founder Nicolas Ruinart appeared on the commercial stationary.

In spite of the standards of quality that were fiercely maintained by Maurice Hazart, the exceptional head cellarman, sales were disappointing for such a reputable and long-established champagne producer as

Bicentenary menu (1929) designed for the Maison Ruinart Père & Fils for use at receptions. The face of the founder, Nicolas Ruinart, is shown above the towers of Reims Cathedral.
Archives Ruinart, Reims.

Maurice Hazart, head cellarman under André and then Gérard Ruinart de Brimont. He was one of a family line of head cellarmen that had worked for Ruinart since the eighteenth century. *Archives Ruinart, Reims.*

* At any rate, the last heir of this branch, to which the Maison Ruinart belonged. There were other branches of the Ruinart family, descended from Irénée Ruinart de Brimont, but they were no longer involved in any way in champagne.

Ruinart. Not counting the bicentenary *cuvée*, production did not exceed 18,000 bottles a year.

The charming and clubbable Gérard Ruinart de Brimont did his best, but he had neither the business sense nor the innovative approach of his father. In practice the Maison Ruinart was run by J. Max Leroy, who had been named managing director in 1934. But in spite of his erudition, even he failed to recreate Ruinart's ancient lustre.

The Second World War, that broke out in 1939, brought the Germans back to Reims for four years. The *hôtel particulier* on the Boulevard Lundy was now occupied, and Gérard Ruinart went to live with his first cousin once removed Bertrand Mure, grandson of Sophie Ruinart-Ouizille, herself a daughter of Charles Ruinart. This family cohabitation, due initially to circumstances, turned out to be of vital importance for the future of the Maison Ruinart. Bertrand Mure was gradually to take on a role that had formed no part of his plans. The two cousins shared the same flat in occupied Reims. The Germans here in the 1940's rapidly adopted the habits of their fathers in 1914 and their grandfathers in 1870, and developed a marked liking for champagne. They bought it for consumption by the whole army of occupation in France and elsewhere. All the champagne producers of Reims and Épernay were faced with a flow of enormous orders that they were obliged to satisfy. The system adopted by the Germans was simple and efficient: at a price fixed—naturally—by themselves, they bought the entire quota of champagne that was not for exportation, in other words 350,000 bottles a week (50 million bottles were exported annually by the champagne industry). The champagne producers negotiated with the *Sonderführer* (military administrator) Otto Klaebisch, with whom the Maison Ruinart had previously had business dealings, but whose presence here and now in German uniform was far from welcome.

The Maison Ruinart was not unaffected by the general business trends of the times. They had to survive, and pay their employees, even though there were not many of them. So Gérard, the last heir bearing the family name*, turned to his first cousin once removed Bertrand Mure, whom he by now knew well. He asked him to help manage and even spend a time in charge of the family business that was facing the

The Ruinart cellars in the old chalk mines at Saint-Nicaise. They are the only chalk mines to be classified as historic monuments. *Archives Ruinart, Reims.*

NEXT PAGE
**The entrance
to the premises of the
Maison Ruinart in
the Rue des Crayères.**

BELOW
**The head of a menu
designed for Ruinart,
showing the famous
Maréchale d'Estrées,
after whom the
Maison Ruinart
named one of its
finest vintages in
1914.**
*Archives Ruinart,
Reims.*

Towards New Times

gravest danger: gradual disappearance from the world of champagne, where for over two centuries Ruinart had been one of the smallest but most distinguished producers. Bertrand Mure thought about it. He told himself that he could not refuse. And after all, it would be a great adventure to manage the family business founded over two centuries before by his ancestor Nicolas Ruinart.

He therefore agreed to carry the torch. He was twenty-eight years old.

Menu — Grand Hôtel

La Maréchale

❦ Born in 1914, Bertrand Mure
is the great-grandson of Charles Ruinart. Charles' second daughter, Sophie—elder sister of André, the head of the Maison Ruinart—had married Auguste Ouizille. Their daughter, Liliane, had in turn married Paul Mure, who was then serving in the army as an officer, but who very soon went to work for Roederer to take the place of his brother-in-law, Victor Olry-Roederer, who had died prematurely. Bertrand was their second son.

Bertrand Mure.
Younger cousin
of Gérard Ruinart
de Brimont, he took
charge of the Maison
Ruinart in 1942.
*Archives Ruinart,
Reims.*

At the end of his formal education, he cut his teeth in the banking world, specialising in the agribusiness. He had a clear idea of where he wanted to go, and it did not occur to him to take an interest in champagne, and still less in Ruinart, since his family ties with Roederer were closer. And later, when Jean d'Aulan offered him a job at Heidsieck, he turned it down.

But circumstances were to decide otherwise. The outbreak of the Second World War found him at Reims. France was occupied, and when the Ruinart family's *hôtel particulier* on the Boulevard Lundy was requisitioned by the enemy forces, he housed his cousin Gérard Ruinart de Brimont, who found himself at something of a lose end. Who could take over the running of Ruinart Père & Fils in such difficult times? When Max Serinet died in 1941, Bertrand Mure started looking after the personal affairs of Gérard Ruinart de Brimont; and then following the death of J. Max Leroy in 1947, he formally became head of the Maison Ruinart.

Bertrand Mure had to start again, almost from scratch. He had to see to the vineyards, the clientèle, the sales network, and the way the business was structured—and during the Occupation, too. It was essential to maintain good relations with the Germans, of course on their terms, for the champagne producers were dependent on them for survival. One of the problems faced by young men was how to get out of being sent to do forced labour in Germany. Bertrand Mure—who had resisted the draft and had refused to leave for the salt mines in Hanover—therefore combined forces with the Eaux et Forêts (Water and Forest Board) to set up tree-felling centres that were manned by the Maison Ruinart's staff and vineyard workers, who, since they were classified as wood-cutters, were exempted from leaving for the Reich. The Germans bled the Champagne region, sending bottles to wherever the Wehrmacht was fighting.

The demands made by the Germans sometimes hinted at their military plans. For instance, in 1941 the Maison Ruinart received instructions to take especial care over the corking of the bottles, which, said *Sonderführer* Klaebisch, would have to withstand "tropical temperatures"; and several weeks later, news was heard of the Afrika Korps' offensive in Tunisia under the command of Rommel.

In 1944, the Allies entered France and the campaign of reconquest began. In mid-December, Hitler played his last card by attacking in the Ardennes. He surprised the Americans, who were trapped by the bad weather that prevented the aeroplanes of the US Air Force from taking off. In Reims, the Ruinarts' *hôtel particulier* on the Boulevard Lundy, now free of its former *feldgrau* occupants, housed—willingly, this time—the *aides-de-camp* of General Eisenhower, who, when he was in town, lived opposite, in the Mignon residence. And the Americans had helpfully started repair work on the Ruinarts' *hôtel*, which had suffered a certain amount of damage at the hands of their predecessors. One evening, Bertrand Mure was dining there with a group of officers that included General Ridgeway, commander of the American parachutists of the 82nd Airborne. Suddenly the weather report announced that the sky had cleared above the Ardennes: the aeroplanes could now take off. The dinner was abandoned, and the officers went to their posts. That evening, Ruinart witnessed a historic episode that was to culminate a few days later in the American victory at Bastogne. The war was almost over.

Seals for Ruinart bottles, 1942 and 1943. *Archives Reims.*

❧ Bertrand Mure remained in charge.

In the Champagne area, the grape harvest of 1947 was excellent. But if grapes were plentiful, Ruinart, in the aftermath of a period of poor business, did not have the money to buy them. So the champagne producers Krug and Henriot came forward to help the thirty-three-year-old chairman: "We will choose the grapes together, and you can pay later." This was a fine example of professional solidarity.

Starting with the network of agents, which he put back in place bit by bit, Bertrand Mure continued the job of rebuilding the business. He made numerous journeys abroad to rebuild the export clientèle, travelling to North Africa, Sweden, Germany, Belgium, and even as far as Indochina and Japan. But the Maison Ruinart also needed new capital to strengthen its financial position. This was the cue for the arrival of Philippe de Rothschild, who was both a financier and the proud owner of a famous growth: Mouton-Rothschild. Mure and he spoke the same language. In 1949, Rothschild bought half of Ruinart's capital. This breath of fresh air did wonders for business. Production rose from under 100,000 bottles in 1949, to 350,000 bottles in 1957.

And if production took off vertically, the reputation of the Maison Ruinart was maintained by further initiatives in the field of publicity. They were the first champagne producers to organise dinners in their cellars—dinners that were eagerly attended by stars from the worlds of singing, sports, and the arts.

Bertrand Mure inaugurated a public relations policy that the Maison Ruinart has followed ever since: the most distinguished names were to be found in the visitors' book and in the order books. Through these stars from a whole range of worlds, Ruinart acquired a new clientèle. Fernandel, Charles Aznavour, Yves Montand, Jacques Brel, Bourvil, Eddie Barclay, Henri Salvador, Claude François, Jean Cocteau, André Maurois, Maurice Genevoix, Sacha Guitry, the driving champion Fangio, Peter Ustinov, Louis de Funès, Curd Jurgens, Gilbert Bécaud, Gregory Peck, and Philippe Noiret. Nor were famous female names absent. The acting profession was well represented: Arletty, Michèle Morgan, Martine Carol, Sophia Loren, Gina Lollobrigida, Danielle Delorme, Brigitte Bardot, Jean Seberg, Geraldine Chapman, Ludmilla

Tcherina; and there were singers, too: Dalida, Line Renaud, and Catherine Sauvage.

But success brought consequences that Bertrand Mure considered to be dangerous—amongst them, the temptation to lower prices. It was essential not to run the risk of damaging Ruinart's reputation for quality by selling champagne that was not the best. Philippe de Rothschild, who in any case wanted to concentrate on his affairs in the Bordeaux area, now backed out. So Bertrand Mure then approached Robert Jean de Vogüé, chairman of Moët & Chandon, the largest and most prestigious champagne producer of Épernay. He persuaded him of the value of having a Reims connection, and invited him to form an alliance with Ruinart. As a result, the Comte de Vogüé became chairman of the Maison Ruinart in 1963, ushering in a new period of prosperity.

This entry into the orbit of Moët & Chandon meant that the Maison Ruinart, following in the wake of its parent company, subsequently became part of the new Moët-Hennessy group, that included Hennessy cognac, Mercier champagne, and later Christian Dior scents. The

Aerial view of the head office of the Maison Ruinart, in the Rue des Crayères. The style and layout of the eighteenth-century buildings (which were entirely rebuilt in their original form after their destruction in the First World War) is more suggestive of cavalry barracks than of commercial premises. *Archives Ruinart, Reims.*

combined strength of their business structures and the benefit of numerous synergies allowed the venerable Maison Ruinart to make progress in all its markets. In France, sales rose from 324,000 bottles in 1963 to 410,000 bottles in 1974. And foreign markets, which were for Ruinart a sort of traditional hunting ground, but where sales had fallen off since the beginning of the century, now picked up considerably. In 1963, the Maison Ruinart exported 110,000 bottles; and ten years later, in 1973, the figure for exports had risen to 781,000, mainly to two countries. From a starting point of 25%, the proportion of total output exported rose in 1974 to a stable level of about 50%. For several years, Ruinart used Moët's distribution and exports network, but in 1977, distribution in France once more became the responsibility of Ruinart's own agents and salesmen.

In 1967, Bertrand Mure, who had until then concentrated entirely on running Ruinart, accepted the Comte de Vogüé's invitation to become head of the Moët-Mercier-Ruinart group. From now on, although he was very attached to his home town, Bertrand Mure had to divide his time between Reims and Épernay, where the group was based. And he was able to devote rather less time to his company of origin, but he knew that he could rely on a team of colleagues to faithfully look after the best interests of the Maison Ruinart. He ran Moët—which had meanwhile become the heart of the LVMH group (Louis-Vuitton-Moët-Hennessy)—until 1979.

Ruinart's production rose to 1,500,000 bottles, and they also used their premises to produce a further 4,500,000 bottles for Moët.

The branding policy pursued by Moët involved organising regular dinners and receptions in the cellars. Companies, associations, and official institutions were frequently hosted, with Ruinart's cellars offering a superb and original setting for their clients' receptions and public relations events.

Ruinart enjoyed a reputation that explained the presence of its champagne at the most prestigious tables: at the Élysée, the Hôtel Matignon, (the Élysée is the official residence of the President of the Republic, and the Hôtel Matignon of the Prime Minister) various ministries (Foreign Affairs, Finance, the Interior), and the Senate. Ruinart champagne was served to celebrate the inaugural flight of Concorde, the twentieth anniversary of the Treaty of Rome, and the Swedish royal visit to Versailles in 1980. And the historic buildings of the Rue des

Crayères were visited by a wide range of distinguished people, including Albert and Paola of Belgium, the Duc d'Anjou, and the ministers Maurice Herzog and Jacques Barrot. Throughout the considerable time that he spent at the head of the Maison Ruinart, Bertrand Mure—being a true inhabitant of the Champagne region—naturally kept a close eye on the quality of the champagne that was produced. It was important to cater for changes in taste, and the public increasingly looked for lightness and elegance, which is why the Chardonnay grape had a significant presence in the make-up of the various *cuvées*. In 1959, Ruinart for the first time developed a special *blanc de blancs*-type *cuvée* which was named after the famous Benedictine monk Dom Thierry Ruinart, uncle of the founder of the business. And from the moment of its birth, the Dom Ruinart was the most prestigious *cuvée* in Ruinart's range.

Apart from adding to the existing range of champagnes, the creation of this new *cuvée* was an important event in terms of the image and reputation of the Maison Ruinart. The Dom Ruinart evoked the memory of one of the most famous members of the Ruinart family, and the shape, labelling and sealing of the bottle harked back to the champagne bottles of Dom Thierry's times.

Two years later, in 1973, a special *cuvée* of the Dom Ruinart was produced to commemorate the two hundred and fiftieth anniversary of the Maison Ruinart, which was officially celebrated in 1979. In order to enhance its rarity value, production of this *cuvée* was intentionally limited to 150,000 bottles, all numbered.

Gérard Ruinart de Brimont died in 1975. Bertrand Mure remains a valued source of advice for several of the great champagne producing houses, and now spends a large part of his time at the Château de Brimont, where he runs a vineyard that includes the famous Sillery growth, all of which is used to produce the champagnes of the LVMH group.

A bottle of Dom Ruinart champagne, 1985 vintage.

❧ Inspector of finances
under Louis XVI, *intendant* of Metz and then of Lille, and

finally finance minister to the princes in exile, Charles-Alexandre de Calonne (1734-1802) was first and foremost a man of finances. And his descendant who in 1984 became chief executive of Ruinart is both a marketing man and a lover of champagne. Roland de Calonne d'Avesnes, of a good Picardy family, was then forty-three years old. His career path was that of a businessman at home in the period he lived in, but mindful of the past when necessary. Having graduated from the École Supérieure de Commerce in Paris, he gained a variety of work

experience in Germany and the United States before doing his military service as an officer in the French airforce. He was infected by the spirit of aviation, and enjoyed flying, hang-gliding, and parachuting. He joined the Moët & Chandon group in 1967, learning about the business through practical experience, and then in 1970 he went to study at the European Institute of Business Administration (INSEAD) at Fontainebleau. A speaker of several languages, he was naturally attracted to the international dimension. Soon afterwards, he was appointed assistant director first of marketing, then of exports. The turning point in his career came in 1984, when he was asked by the board of directors of Moët & Chandon to become international commercial director of their subsidiary Ruinart, where Yves Benard was chairman.

Roland de Calonne, chairman and chief executive since 1994.

He then set about re-establishing a position for Ruinart in the French and international markets that was in keeping with its history, traditions, and the quality of its wines. Roland de Calonne, a marketing man, adopted a three-legged strategy for Ruinart: an increased presence in the French market; an export policy based on a selective approach to distribution and image-management; and communications development.

In France, champagne sales rose by 40% in ten years; but Ruinart's sales figures for the same period rose by 140%, with a record year in 1993, in spite of the economic crisis that had hit the country particularly badly. And Ruinart's market share amongst the top brands almost tripled in the same period.

In concentrating on the export market, Roland de Calonne was merely following in the footsteps of generations of members of the Ruinart family. In the post-war years, Bertrand Mure had made renewed efforts in this direction, and Roland de Calonne continued the work. A convinced European, and aware, too, of Ruinart's role in representing French *art de vivre*, he travelled throughout the world to introduce and represent his company's champagne. He intended to increase Ruinart's presence in foreign markets by rebuilding and motivating a network of agents, whilst always adhering to a strictly selective distribution policy. He visited Germany, Switzerland, Italy, Belgium, Great Britain, Spain, and also the Scandinavian countries, Japan and the United States. Great Britain is once more Ruinart's biggest export market: in ten years sales there rose by a factor of five—as they did in Italy. And in Switzerland and Germany, sales tripled over the same period. In 1994, Ruinart's champagne was sold in fifty countries, including several countries of black Africa, like Cameroon, Gabon, the Ivory Coast, and Senegal; Eastern Europe did not yet feature, although Hungary and Russia made a discreet appearance.

American advertisement for Dom Ruinart, 1983. *Archives Ruinart, Reims.*

If, thanks to a deliberate policy of energetic growth, most of the champagne produced by Ruinart is still sold in France, the proportion of production destined for the main export markets is rising markedly, due to the strength of demand there. In the future, a good part of Ruinart's total production should be exported. A subsidiary has been set up in England, which is the world's biggest market for champagne: from the end of the eighteenth century until recently, Ruinart had always been represented there by agents. And in 1994, a second subsidiary was set up in Belgium, another country that has been an enthusiastic consumer of Ruinart champagne since the eighteenth century.

❦ Ruinart's commercial strategy can be summed up in one word: elitism. This applies to the clientèle, now
cultivated more carefully than ever before. Whatever the *cuvées*—from the classic *R*, launched in September 1984, to the vintage *Dom Ruinart*—Ruinart has a clear idea of its ideal customer: a mature and

successful person, both cultivated and eclectic, with a prosperous life-style, refined and elegant, and a lover of wine in general and champagne in particular. A person who enjoys champagne when he—or she—feels like it, not necessarily in the context of a smart party or a special occasion. The important thing is to enjoy the intimacy of the moment, which is made all the more memorable by its association with champagne. In other words, the lovers of Ruinart are men and women of our time, but who also know how to stop time for a moment, to savour the elegance of the amber liquid, with its fine columns of small bubbles rising regularly: a sophisticated and refined experience.

Ruinart's distribution policy is guided by these enlightened champagne lovers—a policy whose first concern is to maintain the rigorous elitism of the Maison Ruinart. Ruinart's champagne is found only in the best and most prestigious shops and wine-merchants, for example Hediard or Fauchon, in France. Similarly, it features on the wine lists of only the best restaurants in France and abroad. And Ruinart champagne is served at the tables of numerous embassies and ministries, and even at the presidential palace of the Élysée, to mark the visits of important heads of state: the kings of Arabia and Jordan; the presidents of Federal Germany, Mexico, Brazil, Venezuela, Argentina, and Nicaragua; the prime ministers of China, Great Britain, Ireland, Japan, and Italy; and the Chancellor of Germany. And in June 1992, Queen Elizabeth II and Prince Philip, Duke of Edinburgh, also drank Ruinart—as did President Clinton and his wife at a gala dinner to commemorate the Normandy landing of June 1944.

Ruinart nowadays offers its discerning clients a range of champagnes in keeping with the style of the *cuvées* of the past, and made in the traditional way, with the same loving attention to detail: there are the vintage *cuvées* of the Dom Ruinart label, either *blanc de blancs* or *rosé*; and then there are the three *cuvées* of the *R* label—*brut*, *rosé*, and *vintage*. They are all made with only the best grapes from the Champagne region, very often Chardonnay. The vintage *Dom Ruinart* is made entirely from Chardonnay grapes, which are also an important or even major component of the other *cuvées*; with the result that in the Maison Ruinart, the Chardonnay is nicknamed "the dominant grape". The quality of Ruinart's champagnes is also due to the length of time they are matured in the cellars—the historic chalk mines. Non-vintage *cuvées* are never

130

matured for under three years (industry regulations impose a minimum of one year), whilst vintage champagnes are matured for between six and eight years (regulations insist on three).

This is a rigorous process in keeping with the quality and reputation of the product. The successive stages from the purchase of the grapes to the tasting, the creation of the *cuvées*, and the overseeing of the ageing process which observes the rules that underlie the tradition and reputation of Ruinart—all this is the responsibility of the head cellarman Jean-François Barot, a pupil of Maurice Hazart, otherwise known as *père* Hazart, the last representative of a long line of champagne specialists who have served Ruinart. Himself the son of a head cellarman (at Mumm), and the grandson of a champagne merchant, this ex-parachuting officer and enthusiastic marathon runner is first and foremost—and quite rightly too—a champagne lover. He started tasting wine alongside his father when he was fifteen years old, and it was entirely natural that he should go into a trade which he neatly describes as follows: "The oenologist is the guardian of the science of wine, but the cellarman is the guardian of its taste."

Jean-François Barot, the present head cellarman.

Another side of Roland de Calonne's character is his marked taste for communication—an area that is all the more important since it is based on Ruinart's particular image, that consists of *art de vivre* as well as tradition brought up to date. To communicate the brand is to communicate the image.

It was not the style of the Maison Ruinart, founded over two centuries before, to flaunt its own qualities. However, that did not rule out a civilised form of communication reflecting a specific personality. Discretion was no longer appropriate in a professional and commercial world characterised by tough competition.

So communication gradually became a necessity. Bertrand Mure had already made a move in that direction by making the Gallo-Roman chalk mines available for all kinds of receptions whose common characteristic was elegance; and by maintaining close links with the worlds of cinema, theatre, the music hall, and sports. His vision of the art of entertaining was perfectly in keeping with Ruinart's image. Roland de Calonne subsequently adhered to and developed this policy. In good years and in bad, between 8,000 and 10,000 people attend drinks parties, lunches, dinners, and the various public relations events that are

BELOW
**June 1993.
Roland de Calonne
presents the gold cup
to the winning team
of the Championnat
de Paris at the
Bagatelle polo
ground. In the centre,
from left to right:
Jean-Luc Chartier,
president of the Union
des Polos de France,
Mme de Calonne, and
Roland de Calonne.**

so important for companies. And each year, about 14,000 enthusiasts or future enthusiasts of champagne tour the cellars. Ruinart also plays an important role in the communications and public relations activities of companies, associations, and even individuals, by making available a wide range of presentation boxes and objects related to champagne, which are all most suitable for Christmas or end-of-year presents.

Among the various important skills in the wine world, wine-waitering had already attracted the attention of Bertrand Mure, who, in 1979, had joined forces with the French Wine-Waitering Union, to found the France's Best Young Wine-Waiter Competition, which offered the Ruinart Prize to the winner. This professional event first took place in hotel and catering schools, but from 1990 it became more prominent, with prestigious venues such as the opera-house of Lille, the Hôtel du Palais in Biarritz, the Negresco in Nice, and the sumptuous town halls of Toulouse and Bordeaux. Since then, the prize has been presented —after the preliminary rounds that take place in various regions of France—in Ruinart's premises, during a gathering that is now eagerly awaited and that is attended by several hundred people. And since 1988, there has even been a Ruinart Prize for Europe's Best Wine-Waiter, which takes place every two years, and is awarded by an international jury made up of prominent restauranteurs, œnologists, wine-growers, and teachers. Twelve countries took part in 1988, and twenty-one in 1994. Also in 1994, a club centered around the Ruinart Prize was even created, to include all the prize-winners—so that there are now more than five hundred members, three quarters of whom are from countries other than France. To be Winner of the Ruinart Prize is now considered a most prestigious qualification in the closed and highly competitive wine-waitering profession.

Being a champagne that represents tradition, but that also belongs to the modern world, Ruinart could not fail to include sport in its communications policy. Indeed, André Ruinart de Brimont had already established a precedent at the beginning of the century, when he created the Ruinart Prize for aviation. And so his successors set out, in their turn, to connect the name of Ruinart with a sport. But it could not be any sport: it had to be one (or more) that attracted elite clients. The choice fell on golf and polo.

A considerable proportion of Ruinart's clientèle played golf; and so

133

NEXT PAGE
**Homogenisation of
the liqueur-wine mix.**

The Maison Ruinart Today

twenty annual tournaments, each with a cup for the winner, were set up in the most prestigious clubs.

Nor was there anything surprising about Ruinart's decision to link their champagne to polo. First of all, age: Ruinart was recognised as the oldest producer of champagne; and polo had been played for all of 2,700 years. Then the prestigious image: polo was the sport of kings; and was not champagne the king of wines and the wine of kings? As for Ruinart, it had appeared at several royal tables before following the flow of history to the tables of the heads of democratic states. And finally, passion united polo players with the creators of the great *cuvées* of champagne. All these reasons drove Roland de Calonne, himself a former polo player, to make Ruinart the official champagne of polo: every year, the gold cup for the Championnat de Paris at the Bagatelle polo ground is presented by Ruinart. And in 1994, Ruinart sponsored the European Polo Cup that is awarded in Great Britain.

Since March 1994, Roland de Calonne has been chairman and chief executive of Ruinart. Almost two hundred and seventy years after it was founded, the oldest champagne producer is preparing to enter the twenty-first century together with the LVMH group, under the leadership of Bernard Arhault. Replete with history and a rich and eventful past, served at the tables of sovereigns, aristocrats, and also sophisticated members of the bourgeoisie, Ruinart champagne has repeatedly shown its ability to adapt to changing times without making sacrifices to fashion: because it creates fashion.

The light bubbles of Ruinart savour of eternity.

Paris, June 1994.

❧ The Ruinart Taste: a Special Champagne*

The Chardonnay grape forms only a quarter or a third of the make-up of most champagnes, most *vins d'assemblage* being made mainly from the Pinot Noir grape (Montagne de Reims, Haute Vallée de la Marne et l'Aube) and the Pinot Meunier grape (Vallée de la Marne et l'Aisne).

The difference in Ruinart's approach is precisely that Chardonnays make up between 40 and 50% of the *R cuvée*, over 50% of the *Vintage R*, and 100% of the *Dom Ruinart*, which is a pure *blanc de blanc*s made exclusively from a mix of Chardonnays. And Ruinart's *rosé* champagnes contain a dominant proportion of Chardonnays, even though this sort of *cuvée* normally requires a significant presence of black grapes that have undergone vinification as red wines. So the Chardonnay grape is dominant throughout the range of Ruinart's champagnes.

The Chardonnay is a fragile grape that does not like the cold, or draughts. Without sun, it cannot flourish fully. Since the vineyards of the Champagne region are towards the north, the Chardonnay grape is rare there, and all the more precious: it occupies only 26% of the planted surface area. In the seventeen villages in the Montagne de Reims that are classified as *grands crus*—villages like Sillery, Beaumont, Verzennay and Puisieux, all known as "100%"—the Chardonnay grape covers only 54% of the planted surface area; whilst in the thirty-nine other villages classified as *premiers crus*, which range from "90%" to "99%", it covers 40%. Ruinart's *R* label is made mainly from *premiers crus* and *grands crus*, and the *Dom Ruinart* is made entirely from *grands crus* classified as 100%. Delicate, elegant, and light, the Chardonnay allies the strength, structure, body and roundness of the Pinot Noir with the smoothness of the *grands crus* of the Côte des Blancs. For Ruinart, time does not matter: the Chardonnay grape matures more slowly than any other grape used in the Champagne region. So Ruinart's "Chardonnay policy" calls for the wine to be matured in the cellars for an exceptionally long time: three to four years for the *R*, four to six years for the *Vintage R*, and an average of nine years for a *Dom Ruinart*.

The "dominant Chardonnay"—as it is known at Ruinart—represents a particular vision of champagne, described as follows by Jean-François

* GLOSSARY
Assemblage:
*mixing, putting together,
or the resulting product.*
Bouchage: *corking.*
Dégorgement:
clearing out.
Muselage:
literally, muzzling.
Préassemblage:
preceding assemblage.
Prise de mousse:
*the process of becoming
bubbly.*
Remuage:
*literally, being moved
about.*
Sains et marchands:
*in good health and
marketable.*
Tirage: *drawing-off.*
Vin d'assemblage:
*wine made from a mix
of grapes.*
Vinification:
*the process by which the
must becomes wine.*

Barot, the head cellarman: "Our wines are delicate, elegant, enjoyable to drink, and definitely not vinous, heavy, or woody. They typify champagne, and are the perfect accompiament to a celebration or a friendly gathering. They are equally suitable for a meeting at eleven o'clock in the morning, or a late supper after midnight."

To achieve this result, the essential art is assemblage, embodying the concept of taste. Ruinart uses a limited palette of about sixty growths—there are two hundred and fifty growths in Champagne—coming exclusively from the great classical vineyards of Champagne. The art—or tradition—of buying is essential. For some growths, Ruinart has bought grapes from the same places ever since it was founded. The Ruinart dynasty is matched by another one, but this time anonymous: the people who deliver the grapes. No growth enters Ruinart's premises before being subjected to a last stage of the selection process, basket by basket, before the moment when the grapes are declared sains et marchands, and tipped into the wine press. Each growth then undergoes vinification separately, region by region, grape by grape: Ruinart never mixes the different musts. The wines are stored for one or two weeks in metal vats each containing 13,700 litres. Then comes the moment to create the *préassemblages* and the *cuvées*, and immediately afterwards there is a series of tastings conducted in a way that has changed little over two centuries: vat by vat, region by region, and grape by grape. The tasting is a ceremony, and it takes place in the silent and austere atmosphere of a special room stripped of all non-essentials. At eleven o'clock in the morning, when the wine-taster's sense of taste is at its most receptive, a trained specialist can taste up to forty glasses in two hours. The task is to identify and select the primary and secondary aromas—produced by the processes of vinification and fermentation—and the tertiary ones—produced by the ageing process in the bottle. Each taster judges and classifies the wines with reference to the "house taste". A further factor to be taken into consideration is the changing nature of the growths and the years; it may well be that in some years certain wines are not up to their usual standard, even though they come from an excellent vineyard. It is in these cases that the *vins de réserve* are used (between 10 and 15% of the total volume of the harvest); they are put to one side in good years, and if necessary they can be used to complete the *assemblage*.

Vats in which the wines are stored for about two weeks.

The last stage in the creation of Ruinart is the *assemblage* itself. The head cellarman suggests marrying the growths in various proportions and following a strict sequence. So the assemblage of *Dom Ruinart*, for example, takes place in two stages: Chardonnays from the Montagne de Reims, and then Chardonnays from the Côte des Blancs undergo *assemblage* separately, before being married. And finally, the tasters must choose between three definitive *assemblages* and choose the most representative, which alone will receive the appellation of *cuvée*.

The wine is then ready to be put into bottles—regulations lay down that this must happen after 1 January, if the resulting wine is to be called champagne—for the *prise de mousse*.

This next stage slowly changes the *vin tranquille*—without gas—into *vin qui mousse*, in other words champagne. Over two centuries and more, the alchemy of Dom Pérignon's time has become a refined and perfectly mastered technique. Again, time plays a major role: time is the master, and technology is its maidservant.

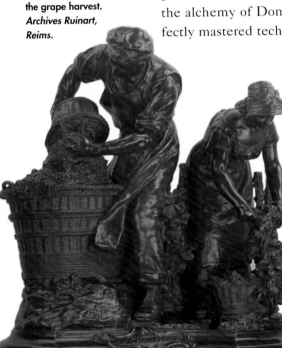

Bronze representing the grape harvest. Archives Ruinart, Reims.

The first phase is the *tirage* from the vats: the wine, first stabilised, with sugar added, then filtered, is put into bottles, together with yeasts, liqueur, and fining additives whose job is to collect the deposits produced by fermentation. A "chamber" of oxygen is left in the bottle so that the yeasts can produce carbon dioxide and a bit of alcohol. The bottles are then provisionally sealed, and are stored on laths in the Ruinart cellars—the famous chalk mines which are one of the distinguishing features of the Maison Ruinart.

There, the *prise de mousse* takes place in ideal conditions, at a constant temperature of 11°C, with a total absence of vibration, and protected from light (sodium lighting is used, and there are no ultraviolet rays). In these conditions, the delicate and creamy bubbles gradually develop.

There then begins a long period of ageing in the cellars, during which the Chardonnay's more complex aromas develop and blossom. From an initial flavour of nuts, they acquire a taste of honey, coffee and mocha.

The process
of *dosage*, following
dégorgement.

During the five weeks leading up to the marketing, the cellarmen carry out several tasks in succession. First, the *remuage*, which brings the dead yeast deposits together and makes them slide slowly down towards the stopper. *Remuage* is done by hand on racks that produce an increasing tilt: every day for five or six weeks, an eighth of a turn to the left changes the position of the bottles. When the *remuage* is done, at the end of five weeks, the bottles are removed from the rack. Next comes the *dégorgement*, when the bottle is opened and the deposit—first frozen in the neck—is extracted without loss of wine; then the final *bouchage* and *muselage*, before the bottles are labelled and packed by machine on the ground floor of the buildings around the *cour d'honneur.*

Chardonnay grapes.

 Ruinart's *cuvées*

R BRUT

Made from a mix of white Chardonnay grapes and Pinot Noir grapes, this champagne is characterised by a golden-yellow colour, slightly amber, with fine bubbles rising in marked and persistent streaks.
Nose: fine and flowery, reminiscent of vine flowers and lime trees.
Taste: fresh in the mouth, round, with a touch of sharpness, harmonious, balanced, and elegant.

R ROSÉ

This champagne is made from Chardonnay grapes for sharpness and elegance, Pinot Noir grapes for strawberry-flavoured fruitiness, and Pinot Meunier grapes for body and harmony. It is characterised by a crimson pink colour, and very fine bubbles rising in very thin streaks.
Nose: at first the nose is very fruity (mainly strawberry), but it then develops more subtle flowery aromas, mainly acacia.
Taste: very fresh and fruity, with a touch of sharpness and roundness.

VINTAGE R

When Nature offers an exceptionally high-quality harvest, the Maison Ruinart can create a distinguished vintage champagne, like the *1988 Vintage*, made from Chardonnay grapes (51%) and Pinot Noir grapes (49%), with a golden-yellow colour, slightly amber, and a very elegant flowery nose: a subtle, well-balanced and well-built wine.

VINTAGE DOM RUINART ROSÉ

This is an exceptional champagne that is immediately identifiable by its lively pink and golden tints. It is made predominantly from Chardonnay grapes from the Côte des Blancs and the Montagne de Reims, which give it its orangey-yellow colour and its very fruity "strawberry jam" nose. It is an elegant wine that follows through its primary aromas with a full aftertaste, and a slightly acidic hint of spices.

VINTAGE DOM RUINART BLANC DE BLANCS

This champagne is made exclusively from Chardonnay grapes mainly from the Côte des Blancs, and also, to a lesser extent, from the Montagne de Reims. It has a yellow-gold, slightly amber colour, and is characterised by a nose that, as a result of the fermentation process, develops secondary aromas reminiscent of dry fruit—walnut, almond and currants. It is full, strong, with an enduring taste, and a marked note of honey.

The Ruinart range of champagnes in the 1980's. On the left, the old blue box, and on the right, the new box. Below, the *muselet* for the Dom Ruinart range.

❦ The Champagne Trade at the beginning of the Nineteenth Century, as seen by Irénée Ruinart de Brimont

Advice and instructions given by Mr. Ruinart de Brimont to his sons Thierry and Edmond concerning the commerce of the wines of Champagne is a manuscript in elegant handwriting that is contained in a large book with bluish pages. Written in 1809, this real vade-mecum it is now largely forgotten, but it is an essential tool for understanding the mind and methods of the most illustrious head of the Maison Ruinart Père & Fils. It consists of twelve chapters dealing with the various subjects that its author considers to be vital for any champagne merchant. The first chapters address purely financial matters: *A merchant's books, Concerning bills of exchange, Concerning foreign exchange, Consignment notes, Interest on money*, etc. Then come the more absorbing chapters, for example *General advice concerning business journeys and the sale of wines*, and *Information regarding the production of the wines of Champagne*—illustrating not only the approach of a professional man, but also the wine-making techniques of a bygone age.

Here are a few extracts from this book, preceded by a description of the functions of a merchant (*négociant*):

"The banker and the dealer (*commerçant*) are involved with wholesale activities. The Merchant (*négociant*) is different from the tradesman (*marchand*): this latter contents himself with selling goods on the retail market, and he knows only how to purchase a bale of merchandise and then retail it. But the Merchant has broader objectives. He is still involved in the different branches of commerce of his region, but his aim is to encourage the export of that region's produce, and as far as possible to discourage the buying of the produce of neighbouring regions, unless it be for the purposes of exportation. A Merchant such as this should be regarded as the man who contributes the most to increasing and enriching the resources of the State. [...] The knowledge of a Merchant must be broadly-based. He must always be quick to sieze all opportunities that might be useful for his Nation. He must also know how to calculate perfectly, deal with complicated matters, understand the value of different currencies, the variations in exchange rates, the differences

The Vicomte François Irénée Ruinart de Brimont. Lithograph by E. Desmaisons based on the portrait by Germain. *Archives Ruinart, Reims.*

between weights and measures, etc. He must be familiar with the different manners, customs, laws, characters and tastes of various nations. And he must most of all offer guidance to the manufacturers of his region concerning the variations that can occur between foreigners, so as to predict peace, war, scarcity and abundance, and to always manage his affairs suitably [...]."
And also:

"General advice concerning business journeys and the sale of wines:

It is perhaps true to say that amongst all the types of commerce, the one that requires the most activity is that of the wines of Champagne, these luxurious wines which are appreciated by the great and by those who like to put a certain refinement in their way of life; which are also bought by wine-merchants, innkeepers, and organisers of public amusements; and which, by their nature, serve to stimulate the imagination of rich and well-off people [...].

On arriving in a town where there is business to be done, it is important first of all to find about about the people who keep the best tables and entertain the greatest numbers, and the people who because of their occupation are obliged to live in a certain style, for example ministers and high-ranking civil and military officers; and it is important, too, to be most industrious in obtaining information about the relationships existing between these people, so as to be able to get recommended through the most appropriate channels.

Since my name has enjoyed a certain reputation for a number of years, and when you reflect that the object of the exercise is merely to offer a few baskets of wine from Champagne for sale, you should not fear to visit even the most distinguished grand seigneurs, who are often not displeased to deal with such questions which help to pass the time of day, and which are often an agreeable amusement for them. This way of doing business is not easy to begin with, but it becomes more natural with perseverance, tact, and habit. You learn how to introduce yourself and how to get yourself admitted; how to have your visit announced by a servant to whom you give your name and the purpose of your visit, or to whom you might refuse to give this information, insisting all the same on seeing his master; and you learn the art of getting yourself

The grand staircase, specially lit, leading down to the Ruinart chalk mines.

recommended to others by letter, of writing personally, and of introducing yourself with the recommendation of such-and-such a person. Always take letters to the post yourself; requests should be written at the foot of the letter, and you can use the margins for comments on orders received. Always stay in the best inns, since they do not cost more, and you can transact business there. In our sort of business, it is important not to reveal where you have come from and where you are going, since the success of a voyage often depends on arriving unexpected.

It is of the first importance to keep to the route you have planned, and not to change it for any reason. If you do, the Maison Ruinart cannot keep in touch with you, you lose sight of your general aims, and the voyage does not serve its purpose.

Broadly speaking, the wines we offer for sale in Germany are: wines from Champagne, white or *rosé*, *mousseux* or *non-mousseux*. The Germans generally like their wines to be sweet, very clear, good and *mousseux*, and what they call *lieblich*.

Above all, I recommend that you leave nothing to chance, but on the other hand that you exercise the utmost prudence in taking orders for wine, not only from traders and wine-merchants, but also from certain gentlemen who are known to be bad payers, and who should not be trusted."

"Concerning white wines

White wines are generally made either from white and black grapes, or from white grapes, or entirely from black grapes. They can be *mousseux*, *crémant*, *demi-mousseux*, or *non-mousseux*.

At Sillery and Verzenay we have always made white wines entirely from black grapes. They are vinous, full-bodied, and their colour is generally brown or stained. These wines should be *non-mousseux*. They are dry and vinous, and expert opinion considers them to be certainly the best wines of the Champagne region. They are generally bottled towards the end of September, through to October, although I have sometimes managed to wait till January. White wines made from white grapes at Sillery, Verzenay, and Taissy are commonly known as *Tisane de Champagne*, and they are *non-mousseux*.

The wines of Aÿ, Mareuil, and Hautvillers made from black grapes as well as a few selected white grapes are generally treated so as to be *mousseux*: they make the best *vins mousseux* and *vins crémants*.

The only essential point is to bottle the wines during the full moon in March, or rather to put the wine into bottles at just the moment when the fermentation is developing. While it develops, this germ closed inside the bottle produces small amounts of sediment or deposits which are often shaped like a tree or a sort of horse-shoe. These two types of deposit generally indicate a strong *mousse*. A white line running across the bottle indicates faulty fermentation, a disease that often results in fatty deposits. The *mousse* is often very violent, and results in a breakage of 20, 30, or sometimes—to the great embarrassment of the person in charge of the drawing-off—50 bottles per 100. To avoid breakage, it is essential to clarify the wines well: they must be fined, decanted two or three times, and never drawn-off until they are clear and limpid.

White wines are fined with fish-glue. When the rate of breakage is the worst, you fear that you will lose everything, and there is a risk that the piles of bottles will crash down: in these unhappy circumstances, the bottles are sometimes stood up so that the cork, no longer moistened by the wine, can dry out, thereby allowing the gas—or the lightest part of the wine—to escape; but in these cases, the *mousse* often turns out unequal, and is sometimes lost altogether [...].

The wines of Champagne are so self-willed and unpredictable that you can never be sure that they will turn out as you planned; often, wines drawn-off for the *prise de mousse* will merely become *crémant*, and sometimes they altogether fail to become *mousseux*. It all depends on the year and on unknown circumstances that you cannot foresee, and which are not understood even by those who have acquired a long experience. In general, it is therefore wise to study wines well and to taste them carefully, and in certain years when the wines are acid, green, and hard, to refrain from drawing-off in large quantities, so as not to risk big losses [...].

When you want to do something, you must know what you are setting out to do, and you must do it with attention to detail; experience is the best guide for the person who trades in the wines of Champagne, and it is best to spare no effort to get to know them, because each year affects them differently and calls for a different approach. You must therefore observe the wines in their different periods, and learn to recognise the different deposits, so that you can take the appropriate action, and avoid the losses that they cause people who do not understand how they should be treated."

The signature of Irénée Ruinart de Brimont.

Ruinart in Russia
under the last Tsar

His surname recalls that of the great poet of the Pléiade, Joachim du Bellay. But the spelling is different: all that Henry du Bellay shares with his quasi-namesake is a marked taste for handling the French language. At the beginning of the century, he was one of the several general agents of the Maison Ruinart Père & Fils. He covered the Russian Empire, which was ruled by Nicholas II, the last Tsar of the Romanov dynasty.

Henry du Bellay would be no more than one agent among so many others, if his reports from St. Petersburg, kept together in a robust black canvas loose-leaf file, did not stand out because of the quality of the presentation, and their precision and scope. The Maison Ruinart's "exclusive agent for Russia" is also recognisable by a sharp sense of observation, not only in business matters, but also in his appreciation of the circumstances of his every day life. In spite of the efforts made under the earlier reigns of Edmond and Edgar, Russia had not become an important market. At the end of the nineteenth century, in the reign of Alexander III, Ruinart's presence was only modest; and having arrived on the banks of the Neva, Henry du Bellay did not delude himself about the size of the task that awaited him. The market was dominated mainly by competing names such as Roederer, Heidsieck, Veuve-Clicquot, Moët & Chandon, Pommery, Mumm, and Taittinger, which had all been in Russia for a long time. But he threw himself into the battle with vigour.

We do not know the exact date of his arrival, but extrapolation based on the dates and frequency of his surviving reports suggest a time around 1900.

The correspondence for the years 1903 to 1907 survives, and its richness of detail allows us to build up the picture of a business typical of its sort, and in a market that was also typical.

As we learn from the elegant headed paper, the offices of Ruinart Père & Fils were at number 1 Nadezhdinskaya Street. And—a detail—that indicates commercial motivation—this same headed paper also carries the russified name of the general agent, in Cyrillic script: Henry

Design for a Ruinart champagne bottle for the Russian market, to be used if the Maison Ruinart became supplier to the Imperial Court. Some of the writing is in Cyrillic script, and the *collerette* bears the Imperial eagle. *Archives Ruinart, Reims.*

Pavlovich, in other words "son of Paul". Ruinart's premises in St. Petersburg also included a warehouse, and the staff consisted of an interpreter named Krietlov, an accounts clerk, and a cellarman whose first name was Ivan.

Throughout his time as Ruinart's agent, Henry du Bellet did not stop searching out business by himself and through a network of sub-agents, themselves more often than not wholesalers with their own agents. Among these sub-agents, Britanov, whose large business was based in Odessa, covered the south of Russia, the Ukraine, and the Crimea; the partners Depret and Bauer—the former had already been mentioned by Edmond Ruinart in 1850—covered the Moscow and Kiev areas; Wittkovsky-Querfeld & Co., in Riga, covered the Baltic countries; and Melck, in Wiborg, covered Finland. Ruinart's champagnes reached a good part of the Russian Empire through this network, which was strictly supervised by Henry du Bellay, who sent letters, asked for reports, and visited or received his sub-agents. Deliveries were made not only in the two capitals—Moscow and St. Petersburg—but also in Karkov, Nizhny-Novgorod (where the Maison Ruinart of course had a stall at the famous fair), Kostroma, Kiev, Odessa, and even as far as Vladivastock in Siberia.

Like André Ruinart de Brimont, Henry du Bellet had a talent for the new art of advertising. He placed—or got his sub-agents to place—numerous advertisements in the newspapers and directories of Russia, for example, *New Time* (*Novoe Vremya*), the *St. Petersburg Gazette*, the *St. Petersburg List*, the *Odessa List*, the *Townsman* (*Grazhdanin*), the *St. Petersburger Zeitung* (the newspaper for the capital's German community), and the telephone directory. He used various classics form of advertising, like announcements in the papers and hoardings, but also the then very fashionable serialised sketches quoting the name of a product: "Before eating the oysters, we had another glass of *eau-de-vie*, and then the Chablis and the Ruinart appeared on the table" (Judged by Itself in the *St. Petersburg List*, June 1903); "Yesterday, at the Pointe, I met a young man who was evidently in possession of a large fortune. On the restaurant on the boat, I offered him a bottle of Ruinart champagne, and then dinner at the Aquarium" (Letters from Paris in the *St. Petersburg List*, June 1903). At Lent, the following advertisement appeared in the *St. Petersburg List*: "For a man who enjoys his food, it is

a great misfortune when doctors prescribe a diet, and when catarrh prevents him from enjoying the delicacies on offer in restaurants. He cannot eat meat, he cannot drink Ruinart—what then is the point of being alive?" Henry du Bellet went further: he arranged for a "Creole dancer-singer in fashion at the moment at the Krestovsky Theatre" to wear a dress-cum-advertisement with a broad band from shoulder to hip carrying the name "Ruinart" in big letters, and in which she sang "two songs about Ruinart".

Nor were the sub-agents idle: in 1907, Britanov put up a thirty-two square metre hoarding at the Hôtel du Nord, Odessa's main *café-concert*. It was "lit by electricity", and in the middle was a picture of the Tchaida vineyard in the Crimea (which belonged to him), with to one side an illustration of a bottle of Ruinart *sec*, accompanied by the words "Ruinart champage, the oldest brand, 1729". And on a more modest scale, the St. Petersburg grocer Andreiev put a large painted bottle of *demi-sec* under a glass cover outside his shop on the Fontanka Canal, in the centre of the town.

Advertising also took the form of the the thousands of menus, sheets of blotting paper, and cards carrying Ruinart's name, that were printed for the restaurants, cafés, and hotels where their champagne was sold.

Advertisement for Ruinart champagne on a St. Petersburg tram, line 5 or 7 (Znamenskaya Square to Admiralty), which went along the famous Nevsky Prospect, the smartest thoroughfare in the Russian capital. About 1910. *Archives Ruinart. Rhiems.*

149

Amongst the hotels were included the most famous establishments in the two capitals: in St. Petersburg, the Cubat (whose owner was the Emperor's chef), the Content, the Bear, the Grand European Hotel, the Hotel France, the Grand Hotel, and the Hotel of the North; and in Moscow, the Strellna, the Hermitage, the Yard, the Prague, the Polkine, the London Hotel, and the Hotel Bristol. And for several establishments in Warsaw, du Bellet had lampshades made that carried the Ruinart coat of arms.

Henry du Bellet arranged for posters (especially the famous *Mucha*) to be displayed in the very fashionable steamboat-restaurants that travelled up and down the Volga: companies such as Kachina, Samolet, Lubimov, Caucasus, and Mercury owned several dozen boats that left from Moscow, Nizhny-Novgorod, Perm, and Rybinsk.

Large posters advertising Ruinart were displayed in St. Petersburg; and trams carrying a prominent hoarding with Ruinart's name in Russian and French, passed along the Nevsky Prospect, the city's largest and smartest thoroughfare, and also along two other routes "through the most prosperous parts of St. Petersburg" (July 1907).

Russian Society was at that time fond of all types of parties and gatherings. Henry du Bellet often managed to use these events to bring the public's attention to Ruinart through special promotions and prizes. On 12 April 1903, the guests at the Polish Ball in the Assembly Rooms of the nobility could drink Ruinart chmpagne in "a magnificent stall lit by electricity" (*St. Petersburg List*); in July 1905, another Ruinart stall was set up in the stands during the horse-trials arranged by the St. Petersburg Horse-Racing Society, with actresses from the main theatres and concert halls serving the champagne; in February 1907, the prize for the raffle at the Ball for the French community in St. Petersburg in the famous Marie Theatre, was a case of Ruinart; and numerous posters and handouts advertised Ruinart's champagne. Apart from what is nowadays called sales promotion, the Maison Ruinart sometimes gave away cases of champagne, or, more rarely, sold at a reduced price. And so, at the beginning of 1905, the Odessa sub-agency, with Henry du Bellay's permission, delivered "a basket of champagne" to Colonel Karel at his property in the Ukraine, "at a reduced price". The present author particularly appreciates this gesture of seventy-five years ago, since the fortunate client was his own great-grandfather.

Never short of ideas, Henry du Bellet even had "penknives-cum-bottle-openers" made, in the shape of a Ruinart bottle, and carrying an illustration of a 20-kopeck piece, "to remind the waiters in the restaurants that for each of the corks they receive 20 kopecks". For the waiters, managers, and *maîtres d'hôtel* were paid a commission on sales, which was the only way of encouraging them to recommend Ruinart, and was common practice among all the champagene houses.

Ruinart's representative in Russia turned all events to his advantage: and so in January 1905, right in the middle of the Russo-Japanese War, he placed an advertisement on the official map of the war that was sent to over ten thousand Russian individuals and institutions, including 850 officers' messes, 440 assemblies for the nobility, 4,500 factories and manufacturers, 380 privately-owned and state-owned banks, about one hundred civil and military governors and chiefs of police, and 200 clubs and yacht clubs.

And that year, in his report dated 23 February, shortly after the violent demonstration known as "Bloody Sunday", Henry du Bellet gave his assessment of the situation in Russia:

"[...] I do not believe that the disturbances of a fortnight ago were the beginning of a revolution, but rather a student riot where these layabouts managed to manipulate workers led by a priest [Gapone, *agent provocateur* and double agent] whose morality had for a while left a great deal to be desired. The great mass of the Russian people do not understand the words "reform" or "revolution", and their needs and aspirations are too narrow in scope for them to make the effort to protest, unless they are stirred up by young people passing themselves off as students, and lacking the patience to wait for the fruit that they covet to ripen, so that they can pick it and then become conservatives in their turn."

Since almost all Ruinart's champagne was sold direct to wholesalers, wine-merchants and restaurants, there is hardly any mention of the names of private clients, and only a few distinguished clients appear in the course of the reports. The Imperial Guard, whose officers were drawn exclusively from the nobility, was present, along with the messes of several famous regiments: the Izmailovsky Regiment, the Semenovsky Regiment, the Royal Hussars, the Sappers of the Guard, the Regiment of the Guard, the Railway Regiment, the 1st Batallion

of the Infantrymen of the Imperial Family, and the Corps Guards, "all young people who are constantly in the service of the Emperor. I am expecting good indirect results from this sale". To these regiments must be added the Economic Society of the Officers of the Guard in St. Petersburg (which worked as a cooperative), the Army and Navy Club, the Marine Cadets Corps, the Navy Officers' Club, the Nicholas Cavalry School. The only unharmonious note was the opinion expressed by the officers of the Atamansky Cossack Regiment of the Guard (commanded by the Tsarevich), who found "the *Extra-sec* too dry, the *Demi-sec* too sweet, and the *Sec* not sweet enough".

Apart from these military institutions whose custom was important for spreading Ruinart's name and reputation in the right circles, the Maison Ruinart also supplied the Prikatchik Club (which Henry du Bellay was to even to join, in order to further Ruinart's interests), the Russian Merchants' Club, the Circle of the Lesser Nobility, and the restaurant of the employees of the Ministry of the Interior. It also seems that he may have received a few orders from the St. Petersburg Yacht Club, the capital's most exclusive and aristocratic club.

All Henry du Bellet's hard work bore fruit. On 30 May 1904, he wrote to Reims: "If one thing is sure, it is that the Maison Ruinart Père & Fils is now known in every corner of Russia, and the doors of all the great merchants are open to us, thanks to the demand that exists and that can only increase." But the Maison Ruinart lacked an imposing title: that of "Supplier to His Imperial Majesty". To be sure, the Grand-Duke Vladimir Alexandrovich—the Tsar's uncle, and one of the most prominent members of the imperial family—had ordered some Ruinart in November 1905, as had his brother the Grand-Duke Serge previously, but however much of an honour, this custom was not the same as the patronage of the Tsar himself.

In 1904, Henry du Bellet started to address this problem. His soundings revealed that to obtain the title and the warrant would cost 8,000 roubles, and a further 4,000 roubles "under the counter", and that everything would have to be done through the inevitable intermediary, in this case a British citizen. Du Bellet thought that the sum was "very reasonable" compared to the rates that were normally charged. The affair dragged on, and came to the fore again the next year, in March 1905: this time, it would be necessary to arrange for a petition to be presented to the Emperor at the Easter celebrations of the Russian Orthodox Church, by the Grand-Duchess Xenia, the Tsar's sister, who would ask for 4,000 roubles for one of her charities, and 6,000 roubles for the intermediaries. And in order to obtain the "Imperial eagles", as they were called, it was also necessary to have supplied the Court over a period of ten years. Henry du Bellet's report pointed out that the Maison Ruinart was therefore eligible, since they had supplied the Court of Nicholas I from 1828 to 1840. No doubt discouraged by these terms, André Ruinart subsequently gave up the idea. But that did not prevent Henry du Bellet from having some Ruinart delivered to the Grand-Duke Nicholas Nicolaevich, later commander of the Russian armies in 1914, in the hope of acquiring his custom.

Russian advertisement for Ruinart champagne, 1903. *Archives Ruinart, Reims.*

On 11 December 1905, Henry du Bellet sent a six-page report to Reims in which he gave a full analysis of Ruinart's position in Russia. It was clear that one of the main difficulties that the Maison Ruinart and their agent faced in Russia was getting the clients to pay. The Russians were undeniably bad payers, and every one of Henry du Bellet's reports brings attention to his efforts to recover both small and large debts.

"The Russians are so obstinate and set in their ways," he writes, " and such an inert mass of conservatism, that dealing with them requires considerable effort and sacrifice, as well as inexhaustable patience."

The report says that Ruinart—"whose quality is not contested at any level of Society"—should continue its efforts to make its presence felt in a country where even some of the larger champagne-producing houses were not selling—or were no longer selling—in the quantities

The Grand-Duke Vladimir of Russia, uncle of Nicholas II. This able man, whose reputation extended throughout Europe, was one of Ruinart's most distinguished clients. Collection of Her Imperial Highness the Grand-Duchess Leonida of Russia, wife of his grandson, the Grand-Duke Vladimir Kyrillovich.

that could justify the "enormous costs in terms of money and wine" spent on promoting their product.

For his part, Henry du Bellet spared neither effort nor expense. In fact, it seems that the Maison Ruinart counted their pennies carefully, and that he himself covered any expenses over and above the allowance he received; and that in some cases he even bore the cost of losses due, in his opinion, to "an error of judgement or an abuse of trust".

One of the particular difficulties encountered in Russia was the pronunciation of the very name "Ruinart". This problem was a source of concern for André Ruinart, who even suggested that his champagne should be known by the three letters "RPF" (standing for "Ruinart Père & Fils"). But this name had already given rise to unexpected problems, since "Père & Fils", when translated into Russian, shocked numerous members of the Orthodox faith because of the similarity with the formula "Father, Son, and Holy Ghost". Henry du Bellet had then got round the problem by writing the French name in Cyrillic script, commenting amusingly: "Perhaps one day they will say in Russia, as they do in Belgium, "Give me some Père & Fils", without having to add Ruinart!"

Henry du Bellet also suggested that in Russia, Ruinart might most appropriately trade under the name of "Maréchale", both because of the famous vineyard, and, he emphasised, because in each district of Russia there was a Marshal of the Nobility; or they might prefer "Brimont", which was not only the name of the head of the Ruinart family, but also of the "place near Reims that had witnessed the famous review in honour of the Emperor of Russia".

We do not know the result of these suggestions, not how Henry du Bellay's stay in Russia ended, but it seems most likely that he returned to France after the outbreak of the Russian Revolution in 1917.

Bibliography

This book is based mainly on material in the archives in Reims of the Maison Ruinart, and also on material in the family archives, a large part of which are owned by Comte Henry de Moulliac.

OTHER MATERIAL USED

Various unpublished manuscripts written by Thierry-Amédée Ruinart de Brimont in the second half of the nineteenth century:

–Biographie du vicomte Claude Jean Thierry Ruinart de Brimont et de la vicomtesse, née Turgot.

–Biographie du vicomte François Jean Irénée Ruinart de Brimont, maire de la ville de Reims, député de la Marne.

–Mémoires d'un Rémois.

–Relevé de mon portefeuille.

–Notes et Renseignements concernant ma famille.

–Brimont et son château–notes prises de 1839 à 1850.

–Essai historique et généalogique sur la famille Ruinart de Brimont, 1896.

Also:

–Bruno DECROCK, *Dépouillement des registres de la Maison Ruinart Père & Fils* (manuscript).

–Edmond RUINART DE BRIMONT, *Voyage en Amérique* (manuscript, 1832).

–Edgar RUINART DE BRIMONT, *Journal de mon voyage en Russie* (manuscript, 1859).

–Patrick FORBES, *Champagne, the Wine, the Land and the People*, London, Victor Gollancz, 1967.

–Jacques GIVELET, *Quand le Champagne et la Chartreuse se rencontrent* (addressed to the Académie Delphinale on 27 February 1982).

–Henri JADRE, *Dom Thierry Ruinart, 1657-1709, sa famille, ses oeuvres, ses relations avec D. Mabillon*, Paris, Champion, and Reims, Michaud, 1886.

–Emile PERIO, *Jacques de Lesseps, la noblesse du vol*, Paris, Athanor, 1900.

Simplified Family Tree of the Ruinart de Brimont Family

Antoine Ruinart
d. before 1638
m. Simone Harmonville

Mathieu Ruinart
1617-1702
Cloth merchant
m. Catherine Bernard

Dom Thierry Ruinart
1657-1709

Nicolas Ruinart
1652-1734
Grand Master of the Tradesmen of Rheims
m. Barbe Misson

Nicolas Ruinart
1687-1769
Cloth merchant
Founder of the Maison Ruinart Père & Fils
m. Marie Saubinet

Claude Ruinart, *Seigneur of Brimont*
1731-1798
Head of the Maison Ruinart
Ecuyer and Conseiller secrétaire du Roi
m. Hélène Françoise Tronson du Coudray

1770-1850
Deputy for the Marne, Mayor of Reims, Gentleman of the King's Bedchamber
Head of the Maison Ruinart
m. Brigitte O'Garvey
Nine children, including:

Thierry
1791-1864
Head of the Maison Ruinart
m. Appolline Turgot
Ten children, including:

Antoine François
1793-1866
Consul de France
m. Modeste Peltier
de St. Michel
with issue

Edmond
1795-1856
Head of the Maison Ruinart
after Thierry
m. 1) Caroline de Vandière
2) Félicité de Lalot
Four children, including:

Arthur
1798-
*Conseiller-Maître in the Cour
des Comptes*
m. Laure de Chabrol

Jules Albert
1801-1870
Prelate in Rome

Sosthène
d. 1891
m. Antoinette de Bengy

**Thierry Amédée Ruinart
de Brimont**
1823-1904
Sub-Prefect of Cosne
m. 1) Anne de Cassan
2) Louise de Touchimbert

Charles Ruinart de Brimont
1824-1896
m. Alice Hennessy
Head of the Maison Ruinart
Six children, including:

Edgar Ruinart de Brimont
1829-1881
m. Mina Sheppard
Head of the Maison Ruinart
no issue

Thierry Ruinart de Brimont
1854-1936
m. N. de Fingerlin

Henri Ruinart de Brimont
1861-1936
m. Pauline de Bechillon

Sophie Ruinart de Brimont
1859-1890
m. Auguste Ouizille

André Ruinart de Brimont
1861-1919
Head of the Maison Ruinart
m. Charlotte Riboldi

Henriette Ruinart
m. Comte Albert de Pelet

Marie Henriette Ruinart
m. Comte Paul de Moulliac

Liliane Ouizille
m. Paul Mure

Gérard Ruinart de Brimont
1902-1975
Head of the Maison Ruinart
no issue

Comte Roger de Pelet
b. 1907

Comte Henri de Mouilliac
b. 1924

Bertrand Mure
b. 1914 Successor to
Gérard Ruinart de Brimont
Last member of the family to be
head of the
Maison Ruinart Père & Fils

Photographic credits

This book could not have been written without the valuable help and cooperation
of Bertrand Mure, former chairman of Ruinart Champagne;
Roland de Calonne, the present chairman and chief executive;
the Comte Henry de Moulliac d'Hust,
who allowed me to make use of the precious family archives;
the Comte Roger de Pelet, who owns numerous family portraits;
Jean-François Barot, the head cellarman,
and M. Jean-Paul Médard,
who helped me to trace a number of documents;
and M. Éric Glâtre, whose idea this book was.

I would like to thank them all.

My thanks also to Laurence Rion, whose kindness I appreciated,
and to Mlle. Édith Houllière (Courtomer).

And a special word of thanks for my wife, Géraldine, who helped me
with the research and with looking through the archives
and writing up the interviews,
and who re-read and corrected the manuscript.

Paste-up and art work by Raymonde Branger

This book was printed by
the Imprimerie Moderne de l'Est, 25110 Baume-les-Dames

in 1996
for Éditions STOCK, Paris.

Dépôt légal: 1996
Numéro d'édition: 7502
Registration of copyright:
54-13-4709-01/9
ISBN: 2. 234.04709.9

Translated by
Sebastian Cresswell-Turner